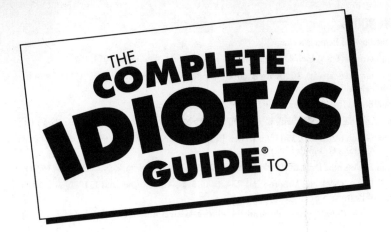

THE COMPLETE IDIOT'S GUIDE® TO

Mortgages

NORTH
5724
CHIC

D0668921

Second Edition

by Jamie Sutton
and Edie Milligan Driskill, CFP, CLU

ALPHA

A member of Penguin Group (USA) Inc.

ALPHA BOOKS

Published by the Penguin Group

Penguin Group (USA) Inc., 375 Hudson Street, New York, New York 10014, U.S.A.

Penguin Group (Canada), 10 Alcorn Avenue, Toronto, Ontario, Canada M4V 3B2 (a division of Pearson Penguin Canada Inc.)

Penguin Books Ltd, 80 Strand, London WC2R 0RL, England

Penguin Ireland, 25 St Stephen's Green, Dublin 2, Ireland (a division of Penguin Books Ltd)

Penguin Group (Australia), 250 Camberwell Road, Camberwell, Victoria 3124, Australia (a division of Pearson Australia Group Pty Ltd)

Penguin Books India Pvt Ltd, 11 Community Centre, Panchsheel Park, New Delhi—110 017, India

Penguin Group (NZ), cnr Airborne and Rosedale Roads, Albany, Auckland 1310, New Zealand (a division of Pearson New Zealand Ltd)

Penguin Books (South Africa) (Pty) Ltd, 24 Sturdee Avenue, Rosebank, Johannesburg 2196, South Africa

Penguin Books Ltd, Registered Offices: 80 Strand, London WC2R 0RL, England

International Standard Book Number: 1-59257-541-2
Library of Congress Catalog Card Number: 2006922336

08 07 06   8 7 6 5 4 3 2 1

Interpretation of the printing code: The rightmost number of the first series of numbers is the year of the book's printing; the rightmost number of the second series of numbers is the number of the book's printing. For example, a printing code of 06-1 shows that the first printing occurred in 2006.

Printed in the United States of America

Note: This publication contains the opinions and ideas of its authors. It is intended to provide helpful and informative material on the subject matter covered. It is sold with the understanding that the authors and publisher are not engaged in rendering professional services in the book. If the reader requires personal assistance or advice, a competent professional should be consulted.

The authors and publisher specifically disclaim any responsibility for any liability, loss, or risk, personal or otherwise, which is incurred as a consequence, directly or indirectly, of the use and application of any of the contents of this book.

Most Alpha books are available at special quantity discounts for bulk purchases for sales promotions, premiums, fund-raising, or educational use. Special books, or book excerpts, can also be created to fit specific needs.

For details, write: Special Markets, Alpha Books, 375 Hudson Street, New York, NY 10014.

Publisher: *Marie Butler-Knight*
Editorial Director/Acquiring Editor: *Mike Sanders*
Managing Editor: *Billy Fields*
Development Editor: *Jennifer Moore*
Production Editor: *Megan Douglass*
Copy Editor: *Krista Hansing*

Book Designers: *Trina Wurst/Kurt Owens*
Cover Designer: *Bill Thomas*
Indexer: *Heather McNeill*
Layout: *Brian Massey*
Proofreader: *John Etchison*

Contents at a Glance

Appendixes

Contents

Appendixes

Introduction

Buying a home is exciting because a home is more than just a house or condo that you live in. It's not just a roof over your head. It's a symbol of success and stability. When you buy a home, you have, in a sense, graduated financially. You've accumulated savings that you will convert into another type of asset. You've withstood the scrutiny of a lender and passed his or her tests on income and credit. You have shown others and yourself that you are worthy of purchasing your home, which over time may store a significant chunk of your financial net worth.

Because your home plays such an important part in your life, it's worth taking the time to educate yourself on how to make its purchase a good financial decision as well as the wonderful, emotionally charged achievement that it is.

As you read through this book, our hope is that we've anticipated most of your questions and offered solutions that help you to become more confident in the loan process. The word *process* means an ongoing action. Not everyone who reads this book will be ready to purchase and finance a home tomorrow. You can be assured, though, that with a little advance planning, any circumstance that presently stands in your way can be easily overcome. And the resulting home purchase will be a better, more pleasant experience for your advance efforts.

Throughout this book we've scattered sidebars to elaborate on concepts introduced in the text. Here's what to expect in each:

def•i•ni•tion

Every industry has its own buzz words and acronyms, and the lending business is no exception. In this sidebar you'll find definitions and explanations for every unfamiliar term you come across.

It's Your Money

Here you'll find helpful tips for handling your own personal financial matters—regardless of whether you buy a home—as well as further insight into how things are done in the lending industry (and why).

Before You Sign _____

If it sounds too good to be true, it probably is. And if everyone who took out a mortgage read the cautions in these boxes before signing on the dotted line, there would be a lot fewer bankruptcies and foreclosures.

Acknowledgments

I greatly appreciate the patience of my family—my husband, Jerry, and my children, Audrey and Eric—as I worked on this book. Their tolerance of my absences and blurry-eyed responses (from burning the midnight oil) allowed me to push myself to complete this project in a timely fashion.

Thanks to Mike Sanders and his team at Alpha Books for guiding me through the magical process of publishing for a second time.

Several colleagues were invaluable as pieces of the book came together. Thank you to Don DeMattio for his thoughts, wisdom, and insight. Thank you to Bob Brown; I truly appreciate his commonsense approach to life in general. I'd like to thank Russell Smith for his willingness to jump in when I needed four hands, Jeff Shaw for his research, and my friends Brian Kemp and Brian Lehner for their Realtor wisdom and constant encouragement. Thank you to John Washington, who continues to teach us all the difference between subprime and predatory. Thank you to Jan Jedlinsky and Cindy Henretta for helping me get my worksheets and exhibits together. Thanks to Eric Westerhausen and Mike Moss—you are truly amazing resources. And a special thanks to Meagan Young and First American Credco for their credit report training guide.

Trademarks

All terms mentioned in this book that are known to be or are suspected of being trademarks or service marks have been appropriately capitalized. Alpha Books and Penguin Group (USA) Inc. cannot attest to the accuracy of this information. Use of a term in this book should not be regarded as affecting the validity of any trademark or service mark.

Chapter 1

Before You Start Looking at Homes

In This Chapter

- ◆ Figuring out what you can afford
- ◆ Understanding the difference between affording and qualifying
- ◆ Budgeting for expenses

There's something magical about owning your own home. The security, sense of stability, and connection to community that come from being a homeowner are priceless to some. Unfortunately, this quest for intangible benefits leaves some home shoppers ignoring the financial realities of homeownership.

So before you look at even one house, you have some thinking and calculating to do. Only then can you set out on the most exciting shopping trip of your life, with the confidence that you are making the right decisions based on the best information.

If you find your dream home first, fall in love with the neighborhood, and start redecorating it in your mind, you might allow yourself to feel pressured by mortgage companies to accept terms and jump through unnecessary hoops. Keep yourself in the driver's seat by resolving all the purely business decisions before you cross over into the dream state of home shopping.

How Much Home Can You Afford?

As you begin to consider purchasing a home, you must first answer a very important question: how much home can you afford? The final answer to this question involves some careful thought and planning. The sale price, loan type, and amount of money you can put toward the purchase all play a role in the final purchase amount, so let's start with how to choose a price range of homes to look for.

There are two (sometimes very different) answers to the "How much home can I afford?" question. The lending institution you choose (see Chapter 2) will calculate an amount, and you will have to determine a number you are comfortable with based on your lifestyle. Both avenues must be explored before coming up with the final answer.

Determining a Price Range

Lending institutions base their answer to the "How much can you afford?" question on guidelines they have established over the years. When a lender qualifies you for a loan, that lender tells you the maximum amount they will lend to you, based upon your credit rating, income, and assets. But just because a lender qualifies you for a certain mortgage amount doesn't mean that you can afford to take on that much debt. After all, the lender isn't the one responsible for paying your monthly obligations—you are.

And your lender's maximum may be totally different than what you are comfortable with. For example, just because you and your spouse can currently afford a $200,000 home doesn't mean that you should buy a $200,000 home. Maybe you're going to start a family, perhaps one of you wants to change careers, or maybe one of your parents will need full-time nursing care. You can't predict the future, but you can try to keep yourself within a "comfort zone" for monthly mortgage payments so you aren't living *house poor.*

def•i•ni•tion

> **House poor** means you bought more house than you really should have. You end up putting all of your money into the house—whether fixing it up or furnishing it—and you don't have money to do other things that you would also enjoy, such as vacations, dinners out, or shopping.

Comparing Monthly Expenses

First-time homebuyers tend to correlate their potential new mortgage payment with their present rent. On the surface this appears to be logical: substituting one housing expense for another. However, there is more to a mortgage than just that monthly expense to repay the debt. Here's a look at the costs involved in a typical monthly mortgage payment (don't worry—each of these items will be covered in more detail in later chapters):

- ◆ **Principal.** This is the amount of money you borrowed from the lender.

- ◆ **Interest.** This is the amount of money the lender is charging you for the loan. The principal and interest combination is often abbreviated and referred to as P&I.

- ◆ **Taxes.** Because a delinquent tax obligation might jeopardize the lender's hold on the real estate, the lender may require that you pay them the money for your taxes, which the lender will then forward to the appropriate tax agency. Taxes might include school tax or city assessments particular to your municipality.

- ◆ **Property insurance.** Lenders require all borrowers to maintain homeowners insurance, also called hazard insurance, on the home at all times. This ensures that, in the event of a disaster such as a fire, the homeowner will be reimbursed for the value of the home. Lenders often require borrowers to pay them the money to cover the cost of the premium, which the lender then forwards to the insurance company.

When the lender collects the taxes and insurance, they are placed in an *escrow account*. The lender is taking future responsibility for ensuring these payments are made in a timely fashion on your behalf. The entire payment is known and abbreviated to *PITI*.

◆ **Private mortgage insurance (PMI) or FHA mortgage insurance premium (MIP).** Both PMI and MIP are risk insurances paid by the borrower to protect the lender if the loan should end in default and later go into foreclosure. PMI may be required on loans with less than 20 percent down payment and is provided by private companies. MIP is required regardless of the down payment amount and is insurance provided by the federal government.

def•i•ni•tion

In most cases, the lender is responsible for paying on your behalf your property taxes and insurance. You pay this as part of your house payment to the lender monthly, and the lender sets this piece aside in an **escrow account.**

It's Your Money

The combination of principal and interest is referred to as P&I. T&I refers to the addition of taxes and property insurance payments to the monthly mortgage bill. Together P&I and T&I are referred to as PITI.

Although these are the most common expenses, you might be responsible for additional expenses associated with the property you purchase. For instance, you'll be required to have flood insurance if the home is in a designated floodplain, and there may be fees associated with a condominium complex or a neighborhood association to maintain common areas or amenities, such as footpaths or tennis courts.

In addition to the payment itself, you will be responsible for the costs associated with all maintenance and upkeep. The days of phoning the landlord to fix the broken kitchen faucet or replace a torn screen door are gone!

And don't forget that the average house is a lot larger than most apartments, which means your utility expenses will be higher than in the past! Plus, you'll have all those monthly bills for sewer, trash collection, and recycling services.

The Desire to Acquire

It's natural to look at a new home as just that: new! And new often means that you'll want to purchase new furnishings, new decorations, and even new appliances. This "desire to acquire" tends to afflict all new homeowners. So it's ever so important to put thought into the timing of the purchases. It's also vital that you recognize the difference between the things you need and the things you want.

When you take into account costs associated with insurance, maintenance, updates, and the never-ending list of "wants," buying a home is rarely less expensive than renting. Some of the expenses will add to your tax benefits of ownership, such as the property taxes and interest paid monthly. But it will typically cost you more to own than to rent.

So before you begin to look at a home purchase, you need to know what you can afford to pay. As stated previously, lenders will tell you how much money they'll lend to you, but it's up to you to know what you can comfortably afford to spend each month based upon both your income and your lifestyle.

The Household Budget

A budget is a money-management tool you can use to assess where money that comes into your household is spent each month. By itemizing your monthly spending priorities, you can set up a plan that will allocate funds to cover your obligations and even set aside savings for the future.

The following form is an easy way to list out your expenses monthly and get started on taking control of your dollars.

To get a clear picture of your financial situation, it's important to itemize as many of your expenses as possible—including food (don't forget that daily latté), clothing, entertainment, and auto expenses. Go back and review sales slips, credit card bills, and your check register so you don't miss anything. Remember to include any contributions you make either directly to savings or through payroll withdrawal to your retirement accounts. You'll never account for every penny you spend, but you'll quickly see where your money goes and how quickly it can disappear.

MONTHLY BUDGET		
Income	**Actual**	**Anticipated**
Salary or wages		
Bonuses		
Commissions		
Interest		
Investment earnings		
Rental income		
Pension		
Social Security		
Child support received		
Alimony received		
Other		
Total Income		

Expenses	**Actual**	**Anticipated**	Needs	Wants
Housing				
Rent or mortgage				
Electric service				
Natural gas				
Heating oil				
Water/ sewer				
Cable/ satellite service				
Phone service				
Maintenance and repair				
Furniture and appliances				
Lawn and garden				
Other				
Insurance				
Home				
Auto				
Life				
Medical				
Other				
Taxes				
Federal				
State				
Local				
Property				
Other				

Transportation				
Auto loan or lease				
Fuel				
Bus and taxi fare				
Tolls				
Parking				
Auto license and registration				
Auto maintenance				
Health Care				
Medical				
Dental				
Vision				
Other				
Personal				
Clothing				
Grooming				
Toiletries				
Dry cleaning				
School and Education				
Tuition				
Books				
Other				
Entertainment and Hobbies				
Newspaper				
Periodicals				
Theater				
Dining				
Other				
Other				
Other Expenses				
Food				
Savings and investment				
Charitable giving				
Pet care				
Memberships & associations				
Sports and recreations				
Gift giving				
Vacations				
Child support				
Alimony				
Total Expenses				

Once you've listed all your expenses, it's a simple process to separate your fixed expenses—such as rent, installment debt, and utilities—from your variable payments, such as credit card debt, food, medical needs, and entertainment. Then indicate whether each item is a need or a want. Food is a need, but eating out three to four times a week might be a want.

Before You Sign _____

When you're preparing a budget, it's also a good time to consider where your money is being allocated. If you have several credit cards with balances, you might consider consolidating your debt. Many credit card companies are willing to increase your limit for a proportionately lower monthly payment, hence reducing overall what is paid monthly. Also revisit what interest rate and terms your present creditors are offering. It's worth a look at the competition to see if you can improve on your present terms.

Next, consider how your expenses will change after you move. For instance, will your commute change? Will you be spending more or less for gasoline? Compare utilities and insurance premiums (if you're paying renter's insurance today). Factor property taxes into the payment. And set aside money in a rainy day fund to cover those unexpected expenses that will inevitably come up, from automotive repair to a new water heater.

Now go back and look at the budget you created, and be honest with yourself. Identify your needs versus the extra things you spend money on just because you can. It's this latter category of expenses that you have complete control over. You might discover that your priorities will need to change as you take the leap into homeownership. Brown-bagging it a couple times a week versus spending $12 on café lunches can do wonders to reduce budget overages. And don't be surprised if dinner and a movie evolves into pizza and a video at home. Or that home-improvement stores become your favorite places to shop. It's all part of taking on the responsibility—and enjoying the pleasure—of owning your own home.

By identifying your fixed expenses versus your variable costs, you should be able to establish a spending plan that will meet your immediate needs as well as allow for some extras. Is it easy? It depends on how flexible and realistic you are when it comes to owning your own home!

Credit Counseling

If you're still unsure about how to get your budget in order, there are a couple of directions you can look for help You can consult a financial planner or money manager about how to set up a household budget. Most of these folks are also in the business of selling products, either insurance or mutual funds. You may or may not be in the market for either, but learn what you can for future savings opportunities.

If you like doing your own research, make use of the resources on the Internet or at your local library to educate yourself on money matters and budgeting. If you'd rather have someone else guide you, many banks and most lending institutions offer credit-counseling services because, as they see it, the more opportunities they have to share information, the more likely you are to work with them when you're ready to buy a product. Keep in mind that you shouldn't have to pay for any of these services.

Before You Sign

Be cautious when talking with counselors who are interested in immediately rearranging your credit for a fee. As we discuss in Chapter 5, not all credit counselors are equal.

The Least You Need to Know

♦ You need to know what you can afford to pay; don't rely on the lender.

♦ Evaluate where your money goes today and determine how a new home will change your monthly expenses in the future.

♦ Decipher what you need for your new home and what you may want; budget for your purchases and give careful consideration to how you are paying for them.

Chapter 2

Choosing a Lender

In This Chapter

- ◆ Distinguishing among different types of lenders
- ◆ Understanding the secondary market
- ◆ Finding the lender that fits

It can be intimidating to explore your finances on your own, let alone with a lender. You may wonder whether your credit is acceptable, whether you make enough money, or whether you're too old to have a 30-year loan. You may be embarrassed by past credit history or even worry about prejudices. And as you talk with family and friends about buying a home, everyone has their own stories to share, and some can be quite hair-raising. It's no wonder that people often get to this point in the process and freeze.

Yet in most of the success stories, you'll find that the lender was the buyer's advocate in the process. The lender's job is to educate you so that you're able to decide on the best loan product for your circumstances. The lender you choose should be knowledgeable about different loan programs and solutions, offering comparisons of why one may be more appropriate than another.

The lender should never be condescending or judgmental. Most important, the lender should speak in a way that you understand. And if you are not familiar with a term or product, the lender should be approachable enough to ask to repeat what was said in "real words." This is why you should interview several people—you'll find one who feels right, not just sounds good.

Types of Lenders

The mortgage market today looks very different than it did even 10 years ago. You have several different types of lenders to choose from. It is helpful to understand where all these companies came from and how they are related to each other.

Banks

Banks have been the place to deposit and save money since the early 1800s, and, in return, they pay us interest for leaving our money in their possession. Banks also lend money, taking their depositors' money and granting loans to others in return. They're paid with interest. So you could go to a bank, deposit your savings into a certificate of deposit that earns 4 percent annually, and, in turn, borrow money from the same bank and pay 6 percent annually for the use of these funds.

Today banks that lend in this fashion are known as *portfolio lenders*. They create their own lending practices according to their own risk-management needs. Often these borrowing requirements appear to step outside of the norm, but still, the bank is assessing the risk and the likelihood of repayment. The approach is perhaps more individualized, and often a higher rate of interest may be assessed. It is like anything else: if it is custom made, it is probably more expensive.

Banks are also encouraged to create loan programs and lending practices that cater to their local neighborhoods. According to the *Community Reinvestment Act (CRA)*, banks are required to make certain that they are encouraging development of affordable single- and multifamily (two to four units) housing. These loans target lending for low- to moderate-income households and are intended to create more homeownership within the community. CRA loans may be offered at a lower interest rate, with a low to no down payment, and possibly with reduced fees to obtain the financing.

def•i•ni•tion

> **Portfolio lenders** make loans, collect payments, and use their own funds instead of those available through the secondary market (discussed later in this chapter). The **Community Reinvestment Act (CRA)** is federal legislation passed in 1977 to encourage open lending practices within an institution's immediate neighborhood or community.

Credit Unions

Credit unions became common loan resources in the 1930s. They were formed to provide services for people with a common background or affiliation, such as an association, a church, or an employer. The idea was to create credit cooperatives whereby members could borrow money for prudent, worthwhile purposes; your character was more important than the ability to repay. Because members were borrowing their own as well as their fellow depositors' money, they were thought more likely to pay it back. An important difference between a bank and a credit union is that whereas the bank is looking for profit, the credit union is nonprofit; it is merely a service for its members.

> **It's Your Money**
>
> Laws are in place to protect you as the consumer. The Equal Credit Opportunity Act, enacted in 1974, was passed to ensure a prospective borrower that he or she would be treated fairly, without regard to race, age, gender, nationality, or marital status. The law prohibits a lender from making an arbitrary decision based upon one's dress or skin tone.

Credit unions offer a wide variety of loan products, including mortgages. When setting their lending practices, they typically lend based upon a combination of their own requirements and the guidelines and standards already set within their charter. Whereas banks that lend their portfolio follow their own rules, credit unions are perhaps a little more conservative because they have their depositors, or shareholders, to answer to.

def•i•ni•tion _____

The **secondary market** is the outlet for lenders to sell loans and recover their capital to lend again.

Some of the larger credit unions are beginning to access the _secondary market_ as a source of mortgage-lending capital. As with banks, credit unions are regulated by a branch of the federal government, the National Credit Union Administration.

Savings and Loans

The savings and loans (S&Ls) of the 1960s had the lending market cornered, along with commercial banks. Today they share the limelight with banks and mortgage companies, but they are still viable choices typically located within your community.

The savings and loan associations originated in the 1930s as a byproduct of the Great Depression. When the stock market crashed in 1929, banks were unable to provide depositors cash during the "run on the bank," so their customers lost faith in traditional banking. People didn't have any money to spend, and so there wasn't any money to encourage growth and development.

The government stepped in to create the _FSLIC_ (_Federal Savings and Loan Insurance Corporation_) and _FDIC_ (_Federal Deposit Insurance Corporation_), which are the federal government's guarantees to banks and savings and loan depositors that funds placed into a savings institution will be safe and available to the depositor. Depositors feel better about leaving their money in the bank because they know that it's guaranteed, and the banks don't need to worry about all their depositors making a run on the bank, draining their assets.

def•i•ni•tion _____

The **Federal Deposit Insurance Corporation (FDIC)** is a federal department for banking that insures up to $100,000 for depositors against loss. The **Federal Savings and Loan Insurance Corporation (FSLIC)** is a federal organization that insures deposits in savings and loans up to $100,000.

As people deposited money, these institutions were encouraged to turn around and lend for residential development. S&Ls became the primary resource for potential homeowners. As monies came in, monies were lent within the region, and monetary stability was re-established. Savings and loans are highly regulated, and the government watches their lending habits closely to ensure depositors' protection.

The savings and loan industry was deregulated in the 1970s so that it could compete with banking institutions. This new freedom led many to new speculative real estate investments during an unstable economic period in the early 1980s. Loans were made in concentrated regions such as Texas at a time when oil prices plummeted and foreclosures soared. The owners began using the S&Ls to fund their own real estate ventures, which were often very risky. The once closely watched S&L industry, although still regulated, ran amok; many institutions became insolvent, causing the government to exercise the FSLIC guaranteed payout of $100,000 to depositors and realign the failed institutions with those that remained financially strong.

Mortgage Bankers

Mortgage bankers are in the business of making home loans, and they typically provide no other banking services. They differ from portfolio lenders in that the money they lend comes from a variety of sources, including banks, pension funds, and insurance companies. These institutions want to invest in mortgages for their return on investment, but they are not in the primary business of making loans. Even though a mortgage banker relies on a variety of outside money sources, the mortgage banker is the lender of record and will close the loan under its own name, so you know from the beginning who you are doing business with.

Mortgage bankers also often service the loans. Loan servicing involves collecting the monthly mortgage payment from the borrower. Loan servicers are responsible for keeping accurate records on your behalf, including noting what amount of your payment has gone toward interest and principal. You contact the company servicing your loan for anything related to your loan, from the time you borrow the money until the time you pay it off.

No matter what kind of lending institution you work with, you should be aware that the loan servicer can change. Federal law states that the servicer must notify you 60 days prior to any change of who and where your payments should be sent to in the future. And during this period, if your payment inadvertently is sent to the wrong party, you will be forgiven any late-charge penalty.

Because they are not lending their own funds, mortgage companies are required to honor the guidelines set forth by their money source, known as the secondary market (discussed later in this chapter).

Mortgage Brokers

Mortgage brokers sell themselves as liaisons between the borrower and the money source. They differ from a mortgage banker in that they research and price loan products from several mortgage companies and banks rather than from a single source. The broker becomes familiar with the lending practices of many companies and can be particularly helpful for hard-to-fit loans.

However, a mortgage broker is not the lender. Mortgage brokers cannot give you a loan approval; they are only the messengers. When a broker takes your loan application, he must forward it on to the money source for approval. And it's not uncommon for the broker to explore more than one company on your behalf, which may lead to multiple inquiries into your credit history.

A mortgage broker is also not a servicer, so when the loan closes, the broker's name will not appear on any of the paperwork; the lending institution you will be working with will be named in the final documents. When you work with a mortgage broker, you allow the broker to choose the company that will ultimately hold your note.

As the broker is searching for pricing on your behalf, he is also keenly aware of who will pay the most to own the loan. It is not uncommon for a broker to place the borrower with the highest bidder. The mortgage broker is paid after he delivers a suitable buyer to the lender and the loan closes.

Lending Sources on the Internet

Although the Internet cannot be classified as a lender, it is a vast pool of information and a logical place to visit as you learn about lenders. All of the types of loan companies described in this chapter have Internet sites, which you can visit on your schedule and at your own pace. Internet lenders provide the same services as do traditional banks and mortgage companies. You can check interest rates, complete a mortgage loan application, and receive a loan approval.

Online lenders usually don't have field representatives, which can be frustrating as you progress if something goes wrong. For example, if your final figures don't match the original estimate, there's no one locally to confer with. Nor is there the opportunity to sit down with someone for a detailed explanation if you have questions about different loan solutions. But, at the same time, online services claim that their expenses are lower because not as many people are involved in the process, and that savings is passed on to you.

Some loan sites, such as LendingTree.com, allow you to fill out a single loan application and distribute your information to several lenders, who then bid on the opportunity to do business by offering competitive pricing packages to secure your business. Whether they are, in fact, a better solution is for you to decide as you shop for the best loan in Chapter 9.

Other Lending Options

Some other lending options are available to you, including mortgage correspondents, private investors, and investment firms.

A correspondent lender falls right between a mortgage banker and a broker. This lender type isn't lending his own money; he offers loan products from several institutions, like a broker. Correspondent lenders close the loan in their own name, as will a mortgage banker, but they immediately deliver the loan to the final servicer, whom they've already identified. In the case of a correspondent, you have no choice of company you will be making your payments to. You don't know their history nor do you know their reputation should you need to call and research your account in the future.

You may find one or more private investors who are willing to lend money to you for a home purchase. These individuals make their own savings available to lend for the same reasons insurance companies and pension funds give money to mortgage bankers: to earn interest on the loan. Because they lend their own money, they can make up their own qualification criteria and charge an appropriate interest return based upon their perceived risk factor. A private source will sometimes lend when no one else will. Be prepared to pay a higher rate for the money, though.

Investment firms have recently also entered the lending arena. A slightly different philosophy applies. Let's say that your savings are held in mutual funds and you don't want to liquidate. Some companies will lend to you based upon your portfolio holdings, securing your assets in return. The advantage is that, again, there may be some flexible rules. The disadvantage is that your assets may no longer be available to you in case of emergency.

The Secondary Market

The secondary market developed in the 1960s as a government response to limited availability of mortgage-lending capital. At the time, savings and loan institutions were the primary resource for potential homebuyers. And when a bank or savings and loan lends money, it takes on the entire burden of that note. In other words, if the loan is not paid, the lender is left holding the bag. Savings and Loans were effective until inflation and growth within certain regional markets in the 1980s strained their resources and many S&Ls were unable to meet the demands.

To make sure there was money available to lend, the government intervened, creating the *Federal National Mortgage Association* (FNMA). FNMA was later expanded into two divisions, FNMA and GNMA (*Government National Mortgage Association*), more commonly known as Fannie Mae and Ginnie Mae, respectively. These institutions were given the authority to issue mortgage-backed securities. An investor could then choose to "invest" in mortgages, which was very attractive because mortgages had a predictable return (their rate of interest) and the mortgage-backed securities were a commodity with an implied guaranty by the federal government. Investors trusted that the investment would produce a return and began to divert money into these securities to lend to future borrowers, thus energizing the housing market.

Like FNMA and GNMA, the *Federal Home Loan Mortgage Corporation* (FHLMC) is a federally chartered agency. FHLMC was chartered by the federal government in 1970 as an additional resource for conventional financing at a time when demand was gaining for savings and loans and thrifts. As with FNMA and GNMA, FHLMC is highly regulated. FNMA and FHLMC are publicly traded and must operate and perform to a bottom line because they are responsible to their shareholders. FNMA and FHLMC issue mortgage-backed securities and use conventional loans as their collateral. GNMA issues mortgage-backed securities with the collateral of FHA and VA loans.

def•i•ni•tion

The **Federal National Mortgage Association (FNMA),** known as Fannie Mae, is a federally chartered corporation created by Congress that provides conventional mortgage-lending capital to mortgage bankers nationally. The **Federal Home Loan Mortgage Corporation (FHLMC),** known as Freddie Mac, is also a federally chartered corporation that provides mortgage financing through the secondary market for conventional loans. The **Government National Mortgage Association (GNMA),** known as Ginnie Mae, is a federal agency that puts together mortgage-backed securities comprised of FHA and VA (Veteran's Administration) mortgage loans.

FNMA and FHLMC are often spoken of in the same breath because their guidelines and lending criteria are very similar. Although they cooperate on a limited basis with one another as they develop and grow, the two organizations are competitors for the same loans being originated by lenders. This competition benefits the consumer by driving down mortgage interest rates.

A final component of the secondary market is made up of private issuers of mortgage-backed securities. These entities are primarily well-known Wall Street firms that purchase conventional, government, and so-called "private label" mortgage programs to be *pooled*, or grouped together, for investment and collateral.

FNMA, FHLMC, and GNMA have standardized their lending criteria to assure their investors that borrowers will be able to repay their mortgage obligations. They ensure a predictable return on the investors' money, thus ensuring a flow of money to lend. For this reason, mortgage lenders who utilize the secondary market resources must abide by these lending rules or guidelines.

Comparing Lenders

With interest rates the last few years at unprecedented lows, everyone seems to be in the business of lending. There are literally thousands of lenders to choose from, and surfing the Net or letting your fingers do the walking in this instance is not the smartest or most efficient way to shop. Remember, this is the single most expensive purchase most folks make, so leave nothing to chance. Talk with people you trust who have recently been through the home-buying process. Their experience is fresh, and if they've been advised properly, they did their homework and may have good suggestions. Also talk with your financial adviser, accountant, or attorney; these people are great resources and often can offer names of local companies they've worked with in the past.

Be specific when asking for a referral. It's fine to know from your co-worker who just bought a home that ABC Company provided great rates and service, but find out who at ABC Company he worked with. Usually a company has several representatives, so if you're trying to replicate an experience, it's best to find the actual loan representative. If you just call ABC Company, your mortgage experience may now be in the hands of the receptionist.

The following is a worksheet to help you identify questions as you talk with loan officers. Before you start with the questions, remember a few key points:

- Talk to a variety of companies to get enough information to make an educated decision.

- Talk to the lenders on the same day. Products and prices change daily; to get data you can compare, you need to get it within the same time frame.

◆ Identify the type of company you are speaking with—broker, mortgage banker, correspondent lender, and so on—and find out who makes the decision to approve your loan.

◆ Make sure you note the name and contact information of the loan officer you speak with. If you speak with two different loan representatives from the same company about price and product, you may get different answers to the same questions. Many mortgage lenders pay their staff on commission splits and allow individual officers to wheel and deal for a lower cut, if necessary, to secure a loan.

When interviewing the lender, ask the question, "How are you different?" and "What can you provide for me that another company cannot?" You may find, for example, a mortgage company gives you a discount or lower fees because you have an account at a bank by the same name. Not all lenders offer the same types of mortgage products, and you may identify a loan product specific to a lender that may be a perfect fit for your financing needs.

And mix it up a bit when doing your homework. Talk with a mortgage broker as well as a mortgage banker to compare loan programs. Loan officers will typically try to sell you on what they have to offer. That loan solution may not be the best. For example, you might have a low credit score and limited funds. Rather than look at a conventional no- or low-money-down loan with minimum credit score requirements, you might find FHA to be a better solution because it doesn't have a credit score minimum. If the only lender you spoke with didn't offer FHA loans, you might never have learned about this difference.

Finally, if a lender makes you an offer that sounds too good to be true, beware! You should find some consistency in price and product, which is another reason to do your homework before choosing your lender.

CHOOSING A LENDER WORKSHEET

	Lender 1		Lender 2	
	Mortgage 1	Mortgage 2	Mortgage 1	Mortgage 2
A. Loan Program Information				
Name of Mortgage Lender				
Contact Personal				
Type of lender (mortgage company, broker, Internet)				
Interest rate				
Estimated P&I				
Estimated escrow				
PMI				
B. Associated Loan Fees				
Origination				
Application				
Appraisal				
Credit report				
Legal				
Closing fee				
Document preparation				
Document recording				
Title search				
Title insurance				
Title binder				
Flood determination				
Surveys				
Home inspection				
Other fees				
Total fees				

	Lender 1		Lender 2	
	Mortgage 1	Mortgage 2	Mortgage 1	Mortgage 2
C. General Questions to Ask				
What is the minimum down payment?				
What fees can be waived?				
What is the length of loan?				
Private Mortgage Insurance (PMI)				
Is PMI required?				
How much does PMI cost?				
How can I avoid paying PMI?				
Prepayment Penalty				
Can I prepay this loan?				
Is there a penalty if I prepay?				
What is the term of the prepayment penalty?				
How much is the prepayment penalty?				
When does the penalty end?				
Can I pay extra principle?				
Locking Rates				
Can I lock-in my rate?				
Is there a lock-in agreement?				
Is there a fee to lock the rate in?				
When can I lock-in?				
How long can I lock the rate for?				
Can I change the rate after locking-in?				
Variable Rates				
What is the initial rate?				
What is the rate basis?				
How much will the lender add to this basis?				
Credit Disability/ Credit Life Insurance (CD/CL)				
Does the lender require this insurance?				
How much does it cost?				
Does the monthly payment quoted include CD/CL?				
If not included, is it available?				

The Least You Need to Know

- ◆ Different types of lending institutions exist, each with their own specific expertise.

- ◆ Secondary market resources such as FNMA, FHLMC, and GNMA provide money that will, in turn, be lent to you, so these resources create the guidelines for the primary lenders to follow.

- ◆ Interview a few different lenders, taking notes to use later to compare services, products, and so on.

Chapter 3

Getting Ready for Preapproval

In This Chapter

- ◆ Making sense of the preapproval process
- ◆ Calculating your preapproval benefits
- ◆ Comparing prequalification to preapproval
- ◆ Gathering what you need for the application

You've done your homework. You've taken charge of your price range by examining your personal finances. You've identified a lender whom you trust and feel is working on your behalf to provide you the best possible loan package based upon your personal circumstances. You're now ready to find out if you qualify for a loan.

There are two parts to consider in the mortgage approval process. The first concerns you as the borrower: are you likely to be able to repay the loan based upon your credit history, income, and debts today? The second part concerns the property you are purchasing: is this real estate worth what the lender is lending to you (in case you cannot pay the payments, and the lender ends up with the house back), and is it a good property to secure the mortgage?

The answer to the first question can be found by getting preapproved to purchase a home—that's the subject of this chapter. The second part of the approval, which is covered in Chapter 11, takes place after you are approved, when you find the home you want to purchase. The lender will evaluate the property and make certain it is a good risk to lend on. This process is known as the appraisal.

Prequalification vs. Preapproval

The terms *prequalification* and *preapproval* are often used interchangeably but have two distinctively different meanings. A prequalification indicates that someone has discussed your finances with you, including asking specific questions about your income, assets, and debt. Based upon your answers to those questions, the lender offers his educated opinion on how much you are qualified to borrow. A prequalification validates that you are on the right path, but the lender hasn't actually reviewed any of your supporting documentation.

> **It's Your Money**
>
> The concept of preapproval is relatively new. Only in the last 10 years has the borrower had the option to apply for a loan either before or after entering into a contract to purchase a home. The preapproval process is preferred by all parties: buyers, sellers, and real estate professionals.

A preapproval is the verification process. A lender asks for and reviews your pay stubs, W-2s, bank statements, and credit report. In other words, the lender verifies everything you've told him.

If you are approved, the lender gives you a letter that specifies the maximum amount you can borrow, subject to a satisfactory review of the property to be purchased. The lender usually places a time limit on this approval, based upon the age of the documentation provided. If more than 60 days elapse from the original approval, the lender may need to take another look at pay stubs and bank account statements, just to make certain there have been no significant changes in your financial picture.

A preapproval application mimics a real loan application, except that you are not yet in a firm contract to purchase a specific property. Following are the reasons why you want to be preapproved before you are actively out shopping for a home:

♦ You'll be prepared. You'll know your price range, approximate monthly payment, out-of-pocket expenses, current market rates, and more. You'll be armed with the information you need to make a legitimate, knowledgeable offer to a seller.

♦ You'll be in a better position to negotiate. The lender will give you a letter of approval verifying that you can qualify for the mortgage loan. The seller will know something about you, if only that you are creditworthy to purchase the home. It will be easier for the seller to negotiate with you, knowing that you are serious *and* have your money resources lined up.

♦ You will save yourself heartache. You will know how much home you can afford so you can avoid looking at homes out of your price range—which means you'll be less likely to fall in love and mentally move into them.

Now it's time to put your preliminary financing in place.

The Documentation

You're ready to put your paperwork on the table. So don't throw it out! Start a filing system so that you're able to produce the proper supporting documentation to the lender. Here is a list of items you might need to provide:

♦ A full month of pay stubs and two years of W-2s to verify your income.

If you're self-employed or paid by commission, provide complete tax returns for two years with all schedules and a year-to-date profit/loss statement.

♦ Two months of bank or investment account statements for your *assets*. If your statement has multiple pages, the lender will need a copy of each page.

def•i•ni•tion

> Assets are everything that is owned and tangible with a cash value. Liabilities are debts that need to be repaid.

♦ A list of all of your recurring monthly *liabilities*, their payments, and any approximate outstanding balances. The lender will pull your credit report, but it's helpful for him to get this information from you as well so he can reconcile your report. Lenders want to make sure that what shows up on your report really belongs to you.

♦ Additional verification that lenders may require, based on your individual circumstances. Here are a few examples, but others are listed throughout this chapter:

  ♦ Divorce decree, separation agreement, or child support order

  ♦ Bankruptcy schedule of debtors and recorded discharge

  ♦ VA discharge of service (DD214) and certificate of eligibility

Although there are industry standards in place, lenders have the right to request what they feel is necessary documentation to render a credit decision. Automated underwriting systems often ask for less proof and are known as *reduced-doc loan* decisions. For a reduced-doc loan, one pay stub and one bank statement usually suffice.

A few lenders have gone so far as to offer to their best clients with above average credit a no-doc loan based on credit score alone. No income or asset information is collected, and there is no additional charge in the interest rate or fees for the loan.

Most banks also offer no-income and no-asset verification loans to help their high-documentation borrowers, such as self-employed clients, avoid the job of gathering their paperwork. In these situations, for a fee, the lender will not ask to see proof of income or assets, and instead relies solely on the word of the borrower. Obviously, the loan is riskier to the lender because there's no proof, hence the higher cost to the borrower.

Income

Any money that comes into your household may be considered income. Your income may be derived from a job, a pension, retirement funds, or Social Security. Other sources could be child support, alimony, or ongoing proceeds received from an annuity or trust fund. Rental income from investment real estate, or royalties from something you have produced, such as published music or a book, can also be considered if it is determined likely to continue. The lender's objective is to determine that acceptable income will likely continue at its current level for a period of time, usually the next two to three years. Acceptable income is considered income derived from a verifiable source, with documentation to show its existence.

If income has not been consistent (such as temporary employment assignments) or cannot be verified because the income is not claimed (as is the case with many restaurant servers), there are alternative means of verification of income (see Chapter 4).

Employment Income

Most of us receive income from an employer, so we start with those requirements. The lender will ask to see your most recent pay stubs, in addition to W-2s from the previous year or two. It's important to note that the lender is looking at gross earnings, not net proceeds after taxes are deducted. If you've changed jobs in the time frame being analyzed, you must provide information from all employers. The lender won't care if you changed jobs, but he will want to determine whether the change was a lateral move or a promotion to a better position. The lender also will look for job growth and the likelihood that the income will continue. Irregular and inconsistent jobs send up a red flag that the income source being used to qualify the borrower may be questionable.

If you have been a student in that two-year window, you may be asked to provide your school transcripts or a copy of a diploma. Education and vocational training are part of your "job experience" and should be considered positives, even if you've not been out in the workforce earning an income. If you can't find your pay stubs and W-2s, be prepared to request duplicates, from either your employer or the Internal Revenue Service. In some cases, a letter from an employer spelling out the terms of your employment may be good enough, but you'll likely be asked to produce some sort of proof. If you do need duplicates from the IRS, don't wait: it can take four to eight weeks to retrieve the necessary paperwork. Contact your local IRS office to obtain the form needed. Even if you've not identified a home to purchase, it's a good idea to have your paperwork in order, just in case.

Before You Sign _____

If your personal situation doesn't meet the lender's qualification criteria, you may need to: (a) wait to apply for a home loan until you can establish the pattern necessary for the lender (usually 6 to 12 months), (b) consider an alternative loan program or product that might overlook the issue, or (c) shop around for another lender who might have a different solution. If you require a special loan solution, be prepared to pay slightly higher fees or see an increase in the interest rate.

The lender may ask about any discrepancies between year-to-date income and monthly income. If your income is lower year-to-date than what you show as monthly earnings, has there been a recent increase in wages that may have occurred, or have you taken extended time off? If year-to-date income appears high based upon monthly earnings, has there been a bonus paid, or have you cashed in stock options? Also, if you expect to receive a raise within the next two to three months, let your lender know. Try to provide a letter from your employer stating the terms of the increase. Those income dollars may be used in the qualification process.

Before You Sign _____

Federal law states that the buyer may choose whether to disclose to the lender child support or alimony income. It is not mandatory that you disclose this income, but if you don't, the lender cannot use the income to qualify you.

If you receive Social Security or pension funds, the lender may ask to see a copy of the awards statement showing current amounts received or, if directly deposited into your bank account, a copy of your bank statement that shows the money going in. If you receive or pay child support or alimony or receive trust income, the lender might ask for a copy of the related decree. Lender guidelines state that you must be able to show that proceeds are being received and that they are likely to continue for at least 12 months. You may be asked to provide a paper trail for child support, such as cancelled checks from the party responsible for the payment. If you are paid through the courts, be prepared to ask for a ledger confirming that you receive this money with some regularity.

It's Your Money

If you are expecting a bonus and want to use it as a down payment, the lender can approve the mortgage, as long as you can provide some proof from your employer that the funds are on their way. Some guidelines prohibit lenders from using a bonus as both income and an asset, so notify yours up front so he can decide whether you need the bonus income to qualify for the amount applied for.

Self-Employment Income

For the purpose of obtaining a home loan, anyone who owns greater than 25 percent of a business is considered self-employed. Because you cannot provide information from an outside source, the lender needs different documentation. You *are* your employer, so the burden of income verification lies with you.

For a traditional, conforming loan, the lender will ask you for the same thing the government expects you to provide as proof of earnings each year: your tax return. The tax return is considered Form 1040 and all supporting schedules referenced throughout the document. The schedules provide the details of how money comes into and flows out of your business. For qualification purposes, the lender may add back some of the expenses you list to offset income, such as depreciation.

Exceptions exist, but typically the lender wants to know that you've been in business a minimum of two years. You will be asked to provide tax forms for the previous two complete years, along with a year-to-date profit and loss statement if you're applying for a loan midyear. You may also need to provide a valid license to do business in the area. The lender will calculate income available for loan qualification by adding the last two years' net income (after expense income) and dividing by 12 to come up with a monthly average. The profit and loss statement is used only to show that you are still in business and making a profit.

Assets

Assets are things you own that have a cash value and can be converted into currency. Examples of cash-equivalent assets are a checking account, a savings account, CDs, stocks, savings bonds, equity in your home, and cash value of an insurance policy. The lender will ask you to identify your assets and will want to see evidence of your money. The lender also will ask you to provide one or two months of your most recent bank/asset statements on all accounts that hold money. If these statements have multiple pages, make a copy of all pages. Be prepared to explain any irregular or recent large deposits other than a repeating payroll deposit. If any derogatory data, such as an insufficient-funds notification, appears on the statement, be prepared to offer an explanation.

If you cannot locate this information, ask your bank or financial institution to duplicate the documents for you, and ask them to sign the document for authentication. Some Internet banking sites can also provide statements. Note that your name, the financial institution's name, and the account number must all be present for the document to be valid.

Also considered as assets are your tangible property, such as automobiles, jewelry, and even a baseball card collection. It is possible to sell an asset or borrow against an asset to secure cash needed for a home purchase. If you do want to sell something, make certain you've kept a good record of the transfer. The lender will also ask you to prove the asset's value, so get a reliable appraisal before selling. For example, if you sell an extra automobile while considering a home purchase, keep a copy of the bill of sale and a copy of the title to show the amount you received and the transfer of ownership. A copy of the Blue Book value or a retail auto dealer's value assessment is also a good idea to have. Paper trails can be a handy way of explaining sudden debt reduction or increases in your bank balances.

IRA Funds

Individual retirement accounts (IRAs) and Roth retirement plans historically are not considered *liquid assets*, although their balances can influence a loan decision. You'll want your lender to know about these assets, so be ready to supply a copy of the most recent quarterly statement. Lenders who lean toward "risk-based pricing" use savings to compensate for other less positive conditions, such as credit blemishes, making the qualification process easier for some borrowers.

Because of the stiff penalties imposed on withdrawals from IRAs, these accounts have not historically been the best choices to liquidate. But if you are a first-time buyer, there is a provision (Code Sec 72(t)(2)(F) printed in the Federal Tax Reports to allow an exception to the 10 percent penalty if you use the IRA distributions for certain expenses associated with buying a home. Qualified expenses include acquisition costs, settlement charges, and closing costs. The principal residence must be for the individual or his or her spouse. In order to be considered a "first-time" homebuyer, the individual (and his or her spouse, if married) must not have owned a principal residence during the most recent two-year period.

> **def•i•ni•tion**
>
> **Liquid assets** are assets that are readily available to you, such as money in checking, savings, mutual funds, and money market accounts. Funds that are not considered liquid have restricted access; these include certificates of deposit, retirement accounts, savings bonds, and stocks.

Note that only $10,000 in an individual's lifetime may be drawn and held exempt for this purpose. To take advantage of this exemption properly, it should be noted on Form 5329, Line 2 of Part 1.

If you plan to withdraw money from your IRA but do not meet the guidelines for exemption, the lender will reduce the vested amount available by the 10 percent federal withdrawal penalty.

Employer-Established 401(k)

Some employee-sponsored retirement-savings plans, such as a 401(k), permit you to borrow against the vested amount. The vested amount means those dollars that would be yours if you left your employer today. The advantage of borrowing against your 401(k) is that you are essentially using your own money and paying yourself back for the loan, usually with interest. Again, be ready with the most recent statements that show your account balances.

Start your research early if you are considering using money in your 401(k) as a possible down payment option. Plan restrictions vary significantly among employers, so it's important to talk to your plan administrator to learn about the features of your plan.

For example, some plans allow only quarterly withdrawals, which means you need to time your withdrawal to coincide with your loan closing. Other programs stipulate that you must provide detailed information on the mortgage before you apply for the withdrawal. In other words, you must have chosen the house and negotiated the terms of the purchase. You will also need to have decided on your lender and negotiated the loan program, and provide the plan administrator with the proper mortgage documentation.

If you withdraw money from your 401(k), you may be prohibited from participating in its savings program for a specified time. Some plans allow you to take out the loan but won't allow you to contribute greater than the loan payment for a period of time. For example, if you contribute $250 each month as savings, but your loan payment is $175, you'll be permitted to pay into the account only the $175. If this is the case, realize that you are diverting savings from your retirement account to your home. You're still saving money, however, because you're building *equity* in your home.

def•i•ni•tion

Most present homeowners hold a large portion of their savings in their homes. The difference between what you owe on a mortgage and what you sell a home for is known as the **equity,** or savings. In a perfect world, when the home sells, the savings can be used toward the down payment and closing expenses associated with the purchase of the new home. This transfer of funds is also called the proceeds of the sale.

Liabilities

A liability is considered an ongoing payment obligation that you have to someone for something provided to you. Liabilities include rent, utilities, credit card payments, and installment loans. Liabilities are also debts incurred for services rendered, such as insurance or doctor bills.

Debts that a lender considers for qualification guidelines are monthly obligations paid to outside vendors, such as your car loan, credit card payments, and personal loans. They are not housing related, such as rent, utilities, and insurance premiums. It's a good idea to have a list of all creditors, their minimum monthly payments, and your balances available at application. Remember to add everyone you have an obligation with, including child and spousal support. The lender will verify your debts by ordering a credit report. The credit-reporting agencies don't always list every debt you pay monthly; for example, some credit unions do not report indebtedness to the bureaus. Court-ordered payments, such as child support and alimony, also do not appear on the report.

Lenders have performed statistical analysis and studied historical data to establish guides to determine whether you qualify for the amount of house payment you have applied to receive. Lenders will look at how much you are presently obligated to pay out monthly and how much more debt you can comfortably carry in relation to your income. Lenders will also review your credit file to see your payment history, and they will itemize any outstanding debts reported.

If certain matters on the credit report need to be addressed, such as late payments or collection items, or if lenders have concerns about your overall credit, you should be notified of them at this point. Lenders should inform you of anything in your credit history that could potentially keep you from getting a loan. Lenders should openly discuss all items with you pertaining to the report and should offer suggestions on how to correct anything. You may be asked to write a letter of explanation addressing issues such as late payments, derogatory history, or new accounts. It's not unusual to find discrepancies on the report, and you may be asked to clarify, explain, or assist in the removal of something that was not correctly reported.

It's Your Money

If you've received your credit report recently, let your lender know! She can sometimes answer general questions by viewing your report. She will need to eventually pull her own report, however, because the Credit Reporting Act/Right to Privacy states that only the party requesting the report has access to the information.

Other Verifications

You may be asked to provide evidence of satisfactory rental payments to a present or previous landlord. Compile the last 12 months of cancelled checks (or bank statements showing the monthly debit if you do not receive the checks), or the name and address of the landlord so the bank can verify rental history. It's also a good idea any time you're trying to establish your creditworthiness to ask for letters of recommendations from your landlord or anyone else you have paid monthly installments to for a service or product, such as a dentist or utility company.

If funds are coming from a source other than savings, you will be asked to provide evidence of cash to close. Gifts are common sources of funds for a home purchase. The documentation needed to verify the gift varies depending on the type of loan you are applying for, but you will almost always need to have a gift letter stating that the donor is giving you this money and not expecting it to be repaid. You may also need a copy of the donor's check to you and a copy of the deposit slip when you put it into your bank account. In some cases, you may be asked to provide evidence that the donor actually had the money to give to you. It's important that you openly discuss the source of funds with your lender because some loans require that the borrower contribute a certain amount or percentage of his or her own funds to the purchase. And as we mentioned, a large deposit on your bank statement will trigger the question anyway.

If you were recently divorced, you may be asked to provide a copy of your divorce decree as evidence of any obligations associated with that separation, such as child support, alimony, or separate maintenance.

If you recently underwent bankruptcy, you may be asked for copies of the bankruptcy schedules, along with a copy of the discharge of debtor. You may also be asked to provide a letter explaining the circumstances surrounding the bankruptcy. Loan options after a bankruptcy are handled individually, based upon the type of bankruptcy, the cause and ultimate resolution, and the time since the completion of the action.

It's Your Money

A quitclaim deed may be filed to remove a party from his or her ownership, perhaps due to a divorce or separation. This document releases the borrower's interest, or claim to the property. It does not change the existing mortgage. If the mortgage loan goes into default, the lender may try to recover damages from all borrowers whose names appear on the mortgage. The only way to eliminate your obligation totally is to refinance, removing yourself from the loan entirely.

Low- or No-Documentation Loans

As mentioned earlier in the chapter, other loans are available if you can't find all of the papers you need or if you just want to avoid the hassle of pulling together what's typically required.

No-documentation loans usually involve a minimum down payment of 20 percent and require excellent compensating factors, including good credit. You can expect extra fees and a higher interest rate, based upon what documentation you do and don't want to give to the lender. For example, you could pay as much as 2 percent higher in interest for the luxury of not disclosing your income.

Here is a list of loans and their documentation requirements:

♦ **No income.** You must have a job for most of these loans, but you do not have to state your earnings. The income section is left blank and ratios are not calculated. If bank statements are used to verify the assets on these loans and they reflect even interest income, the interest income must be blacked out.

- ◆ **No asset.** You do not list where your money resides on the application.

- ◆ **No income/no asset.** Also known as NINA, no income information is noted, nor are assets listed. An employer must be listed, and some lenders require a minimum time on the job, such as two years.

- ◆ **Stated income.** Income is noted on the application but is not verified. An employer is listed but may or may not be called.

- ◆ **Stated income/stated asset.** Also known as SISA. Income and assets are on the credit report, but no supporting documentation is collected.

In all cases when income is stated, it must be deemed reasonable for the occupation. For example, it may be questioned if a pizza delivery driver states $5,000 a month in income.

It's also important to note that when lenders offer these loan options, they're relying on the buyer to be truthful. The reduced documentation and stated loans are for your convenience; they're not meant to allow you to commit fraud. For some loan types, you will be asked to sign an IRS Form 4509, which authorizes an auditor to request a copy of anything you've provided as it relates to your income tax return.

Every loan is potentially audited, by both the lender and various government regulatory agencies. In fact, one out of eight loans is reviewed after closing. The audit is done to make certain no fraud was committed on the loan and that the lender has complied with all federal disclosure laws.

Now that you've learned what you need and what you can do without as far as documents, it's time to complete the loan application in Chapter 4.

The Least You Need to Know

- ◆ The preapproval process is meant to take the guesswork out of purchasing a home; you will be fully aware of fees, payments, and how much home to look at before you become emotionally attached to something out of your price range.

◆ The lender will ask you to provide detailed information and documentation regarding your income assets and debt, so take time to compile the proper paperwork—and be prepared for a barrage of questions.

◆ Some loans do not require that the lender see evidence of income and assets, but you must have excellent credit and be prepared to pay more for these loans because they are riskier to the lender.

Chapter 4

Completing the Loan Application

In This Chapter

◆ Completing a loan application

◆ Making sense of application form 1003

◆ Understanding underwriting processes and procedures

◆ Knowing what to expect from the application process

When you have your pay stubs, W-2 forms, bank statements, and miscellaneous documents on hand, you are ready to proceed with the mortgage application. The application can be completed any number of ways: by mail, face to face, by telephone, or via the Internet. Regardless of how you want to provide this information, lenders are required by law to disclose how the information was obtained.

Application Form 1003

The Residential Loan Application, also known by its form number 1003 is a standard form, used by lenders from coast to coast. A copy of the application is included in this chapter. As you'll see, it's a simple form that you can complete on your own. Still, most borrowers elect to have the lender complete the form because it's a more efficient way for the lender to begin to identify a loan solution for you.

If you intend to enlist the help of a lender to complete the form, plan to make an appointment. The loan officer will conduct an interview either in person or on the telephone.

The Uniform Residential Mortgage Application, Form #1003

The residential mortgage application is divided into 10 sections. Here is a brief overview of each section and what information is required to complete the document:

Section I. Type of Mortgage and Terms of Loan: Indicate the type of loan applied for and the term of the mortgage, the interest rate, and the amount borrowed.

Section II. Property Information and Purpose of Loan: List the property address of the home to be mortgaged, along with the age of the home. You choose here how you want to hold the title or take ownership of the property. This is where you note whether it's a single-family or multifamily home, existing or new construction, and a purchase or refinance.

Section III. Borrower Information: This personal information is used for contact and reference purposes. The information provided in this section is used to order the credit report, so it's essential that you provide accurate information.

Section IV. Employment Information: List where you work and for how long, your job title, and how much you've earned monthly. You will be asked to provide two years' worth of history.

Uniform Residential Loan Application

This application is designed to be completed by the applicant(s) with the Lender's assistance. Applicants should complete this form as "Borrower" or "Co-Borrower", as applicable. Co-Borrower information must also be provided (and the appropriate box checked) when ☐ the income or assets of a person other than the "Borrower" (including the Borrower's spouse) will be used as a basis for loan qualification or ☐ the income or assets of the Borrower's spouse will not be used as a basis for loan qualification, but his or her liabilities must be considered because the Borrower resides in a community property state, the security property is located in a community property state, or the Borrower is relying on other property located in a community property state as a basis for repayment of the loan.

I. TYPE OF MORTGAGE AND TERMS OF LOAN

Mortgage Applied for:	☐ VA ☐ Conventional ☐ Other (explain): ☐ FHA ☐ USDA/Rural Housing Service	Agency Case Number	Lender Case Number

Amount $	Interest Rate %	No. of Months	Amortization Type:	☐ Fixed Rate ☐ Other (explain): ☐ GPM ☐ ARM (type):

II. PROPERTY INFORMATION AND PURPOSE OF LOAN

Subject Property Address (street, city, state, ZIP)	No. of Units

Legal Description of Subject Property (attach description if necessary)	Year Built

Purpose of Loan ☐ Purchase ☐ Construction ☐ Other (explain): ☐ Refinance ☐ Construction-Permanent	Property will be: ☐ Primary Residence ☐ Secondary Residence ☐ Investment

Complete this line if construction or construction-permanent loan.

Year Lot Acquired	Original Cost $	Amount Existing Liens $	(a) Present Value of Lot $	(b) Cost of Improvements $	Total (a+b) $

Complete this line if this is a refinance loan.

Year Acquired	Original Cost $	Amount Existing Liens $	Purpose of Refinance	Describe Improvements ☐ made ☐ to be made Cost: $

Title will be held in what Name(s)	Manner in which Title will be held	Estate will be held in: ☑ Fee Simple ☐ Leasehold (show expiration date)

Source of Down Payment, Settlement Charges and/or Subordinate Financing (explain)		

III. BORROWER INFORMATION

Borrower	Co-Borrower
Borrower's Name (include Jr. or Sr. if applicable)	Co-Borrower's Name (include Jr. or Sr. if applicable)

Social Security Number	Home Phone (incl. area code)	DOB (MM/DD/YYYY)	Yrs. School	Social Security Number	Home Phone (incl. area code)	DOB (MM/DD/YYYY)	Yrs. School

☐ Married ☐ Unmarried (include single, ☐ Separated divorced, widowed)	Dependents (not listed by Co-Borrower) no. ages	☐ Married ☐ Unmarried (include single, ☐ Separated divorced, widowed)	Dependents (not listed by Borrower) no. ages

Present Address (street, city, state, ZIP) ☐ Own ☐ Rent ____No. Yrs.	Present Address (street, city, state, ZIP) ☐ Own ☐ Rent ____No. Yrs.

Mailing Address, if different from Present Address	Mailing Address, if different from Present Address

If residing at present address for less than two years, complete the following:

Former Address (street, city, state, ZIP) ☐ Own ☐ Rent ____No. Yrs.	Former Address (street, city, state, ZIP) ☐ Own ☐ Rent ____No. Yrs.

IV. EMPLOYMENT INFORMATION

Borrower		Co-Borrower	
Name & Address of Employer ☐ Self Employed	Yrs. on this job	Name & Address of Employer ☐ Self Employed	Yrs. on this job
	Yrs. employed in this line of work/profession		Yrs. employed in this line of work/profession
Position/Title/Type of Business	Business Phone (incl. area code)	Position/Title/Type of Business	Business Phone (incl. area code)

If employed in current position for less than two years or if currently employed in more than one position, complete the following:

Name & Address of Employer ☐ Self Employed	Dates (from-to)	Name & Address of Employer ☐ Self Employed	Dates (from-to)
	Monthly Income $		Monthly Income $
Position/Title/Type of Business	Business Phone (incl. area code)	Position/Title/Type of Business	Business Phone (incl. area code)

Name & Address of Employer ☐ Self Employed	Dates (from-to)	Name & Address of Employer ☐ Self Employed	Dates (from-to)
	Monthly Income $		Monthly Income $
Position/Title/Type of Business	Business Phone (incl. area code)	Position/Title/Type of Business	Business Phone (incl. area code)

V. MONTHLY INCOME AND COMBINED HOUSING EXPENSE INFORMATION

Gross Monthly Income	Borrower	Co-Borrower	Total	Combined Monthly Housing Expense	Present	Proposed
Base Empl. Income*	$	$	$	Rent	$	
Overtime				First Mortgage (P&I)		$
Bonuses				Other Financing (P&I)		
Commissions				Hazard Insurance		
Dividends/Interest				Real Estate Taxes		
Net Rental Income				Mortgage Insurance		
Other (before completing, see the notice in "describe other income," below)				Homeowner Assn. Dues		
				Other:		
Total	$	$	$	Total	$	$

* Self Employed Borrower(s) may be required to provide additional documentation such as tax returns and financial statements.

Describe Other Income *Notice:* Alimony, child support, or separate maintenance income need not be revealed if the Borrower (B) or Co-Borrower (C) does not choose to have it considered for repaying this loan.

B/C		Monthly Amount
		$

VI. ASSETS AND LIABILITIES

This Statement and any applicable supporting schedules may be completed jointly by both married and unmarried Co-borrowers if their assets and liabilities are sufficiently joined so that the Statement can be meaningfully and fairly presented on a combined basis; otherwise, separate Statements and Schedules are required. If the Co-Borrower section was completed about a spouse, this Statement and supporting schedules must be completed about that spouse also.

Completed ☐ Jointly ☐ Not Jointly

ASSETS Description	Cash or Market Value	Liabilities and Pledged Assets. List the creditor's name, address and account number for all outstanding debts, including automobile loans, revolving charge accounts, real estate loans, alimony, child support, stock pledges, etc. Use continuation sheet, if necessary. Indicate by (*) those liabilities which will be satisfied upon sale of real estate owned or upon refinancing of the subject property.		
Cash deposit toward purchase held by: $		LIABILITIES	Monthly Payment & Months Left to Pay	Unpaid Balance
List checking and savings accounts below		Name and address of Company	$ Payment/Months	$
Name and address of Bank, S&L, or Credit Union				
		Acct. no.		
Acct. no. $		Name and address of Company	$ Payment/Months	$
Name and address of Bank, S&L, or Credit Union				
		Acct. no.		
Acct. no. $		Name and address of Company	$ Payment/Months	$
Name and address of Bank, S&L, or Credit Union				
		Acct. no.		
Acct. no. $		Name and address of Company	$ Payment/Months	$
Name and address of Bank, S&L, or Credit Union				
		Acct. no.		
Acct. no. $		Name and address of Company	$ Payment/Months	$
Stocks & Bonds (Company name/ number & description) $				
		Acct. no.		
		Name and address of Company	$ Payment/Months	$
Life insurance net cash value $				
Face amount: $				
Subtotal Liquid Assets $		Acct. no.		
Real estate owned (enter market value from schedule of real estate owned) $		Name and address of Company	$ Payment/Months	$
Vested interest in retirement fund $				
Net worth of business(es) owned (attach financial statement) $				
Automobiles owned (make and year) $		Acct. no.		
		Alimony/Child Support/Separate Maintenance Payments Owed to:	$	
Other Assets (itemize) $				
PERSONAL PROPERTY		Job Related Expense (child care, union dues, etc.)	$	
		Total Monthly Payments	$	
Total Assets a. $		Net Worth (a minus b) => $	**Total Liabilities b.** $	

VI. ASSETS AND LIABILITIES (cont.)							

Schedule of Real Estate Owned (if additional properties are owned, use continuation sheet)

Property Address (enter S if sold, PS if pending sale or R if rental being held for income)	Type of Property	Present Market Value	Amount of Mortgages & Liens	Gross Rental Income	Mortgage Payments	Insurance, Maintenance, Taxes & Misc.	Net Rental Income
		$	$	$	$	$	$
	Totals	$	$	$	$	$	$

List any additional names under which credit has previously been received and indicate appropriate creditor name(s) and account number(s):

Alternate Name	Creditor Name	Account Number

VII. DETAILS OF TRANSACTION		VIII. DECLARATIONS				
a. Purchase price	$	If you answer "yes" to any questions a through i, please use continuation sheet for explanation.				
			Borrower		Co-Borrower	
b. Alterations, improvements, repairs			Yes	No	Yes	No
c. Land (if acquired separately)		a. Are there any outstanding judgments against you?	☐	☐	☐	☐
d. Refinance (incl. debts to be paid off)		b. Have you been declared bankrupt within the past 7 years?	☐	☐	☐	☐
e. Estimated prepaid items		c. Have you had property foreclosed upon or given title or deed in lieu thereof in the last 7 years?	☐	☐	☐	☐
f. Estimated closing costs						
g. PMI, MIP, Funding Fee		d. Are you a party to a lawsuit?	☐	☐	☐	☐
h. Discount (if Borrower will pay)		e. Have you directly or indirectly been obligated on any loan which resulted in foreclosure, transfer of title in lieu of foreclosure, or judgment?	☐	☐	☐	☐
i. Total costs (add items a through h)		(This would include such loans as home mortgage loans, SBA loans, home improvement loans, educational loans, manufactured (mobile) home loans, any mortgage, financial obligation, bond, or loan guarantee. If "Yes," provide details, including date, name and address of Lender, FHA or VA case number, if any, and reasons for the action.)				
j. Subordinate financing						
k. Borrower's closing costs paid by Seller						
l. Other Credits(explain)		f. Are you presently delinquent or in default on any Federal debt or any other loan, mortgage, financial obligation, bond, or loan guarantee? If "Yes," give details as described in the preceding question.	☐	☐	☐	☐
		g. Are you obligated to pay alimony, child support, or separate maintenance?	☐	☐	☐	☐
		h. Is any part of the down payment borrowed?	☐	☐	☐	☐
		i. Are you a co-maker or endorser on a note?	☐	☐	☐	☐
		j. Are you a U. S. citizen?	☐	☐	☐	☐
m. Loan amount (exclude PMI, MIP, Funding Fee financed)		k. Are you a permanent resident alien?	☐	☐	☐	☐
		l. Do you intend to occupy the property as your primary residence? If "Yes," complete question m below.	☐	☐	☐	☐
n. PMI, MIP, Funding Fee financed		m. Have you had an ownership interest in a property in the last three years?	☐	☐	☐	☐
o. Loan amount (add m & n)		(1) What type of property did you own-principal residence (PR), second home (SH), or investment property (IP)?				
p. Cash from/to Borrower (subtract j, k, l & o from i)		(2) How did you hold title to the home-solely by yourself (S), jointly with your spouse (SP), or jointly with another person (O)?				

IX. ACKNOWLEDGMENT AND AGREEMENT

Each of the undersigned specifically represents to Lender and to Lender's actual or potential agents, brokers, processors, attorneys, insurers, servicers, successors and assigns and agrees and acknowledges that: (1) the information provided in this application is true and correct as of the date set forth opposite my signature and that any intentional or negligent misrepresentation of this information contained in this application may result in civil liability, including monetary damages, to any person who may suffer any loss due to reliance upon any misrepresentation that I have made on this application, and/or in criminal penalties including, but not limited to, fine or imprisonment or both under the provisions of Title 18, United States Code, Sec. 1001, et seq.; (2) the loan requested pursuant to this application (the "Loan") will be secured by a mortgage or deed of trust on the property described herein; (3) the property will not be used for any illegal or prohibited purpose or use; (4) all statements made in this application are made for the purpose of obtaining a residential mortgage loan; (5) the property will be occupied as indicated herein; (6) any owner or servicer of the Loan may verify or reverify any information contained in the application from any source named in this application, and Lender, its successors or assigns may retain the original and/or an electronic record of this application, even if the Loan is not approved; (7) the Lender and its agents, brokers, insurers, servicers, successors and assigns may continuously rely on the information contained in the application, and I am obligated to amend and/or supplement the information provided in this application if any of the material facts that I have represented herein should change prior to closing of the Loan; (8) in the event that my payments on the Loan become delinquent, the owner or servicer of the Loan may, in addition to any other rights and remedies that it may have relating to such delinquency, report my name and account information to one or more consumer credit reporting agencies; (9) ownership of the Loan and/or administration of the Loan account may be transferred with such notice as may be required by law; (10) neither Lender nor its agents, brokers, insurers, servicers, successors or assigns has made any representation or warranty, express or implied, to me regarding the property or the condition or value of the property; and (11) my transmission of this application as an "electronic record" containing my "electronic signature," as those terms are defined in applicable federal and/or state laws (excluding audio and video recordings), or my facsimile transmission of this application containing a facsimile of my signature, shall be as effective, enforceable and valid as if a paper version of this application were delivered containing my original written signature.

Borrower's Signature	Date	Co-Borrower's Signature	Date
X		X	

X. INFORMATION FOR GOVERNMENT MONITORING PURPOSES

The following information is requested by the Federal Government for certain types of loans related to a dwelling in order to monitor the lender's compliance with equal credit opportunity, fair housing and home mortgage disclosure laws. You are not required to furnish this information, but are encouraged to do so. The law provides that a Lender may discriminate neither on the basis of this information, nor on whether you choose to furnish it. If you furnish the information, please provide both ethnicity and race. For race, you may check more than one designation. If you do not furnish ethnicity, race, or sex, under Federal regulations, this lender is required to note the information on the basis of visual observation or surname. If you do not wish to furnish the information, please check the box below. (Lender must review the above material to assure that the disclosures satisfy all requirements to which the lender is subject under applicable state law for the particular type of loan applied for.)

BORROWER ☐ I do not wish to furnish this information			CO-BORROWER ☐ I do not wish to furnish this information		
Ethnicity:	☐ Hispanic or Latino	☐ Not Hispanic or Latino	**Ethnicity:**	☐ Hispanic or Latino	☐ Not Hispanic or Latino
Race:	☐ American Indian or Alaska Native　☐ Asian	☐ Black or African American	**Race:**	☐ American Indian or Alaska Native　☐ Asian	☐ Black or African American
	☐ Native Hawaiian or Other Pacific Islander	☐ White		☐ Native Hawaiian or Other Pacific Islander	☐ White
Sex:	☐ Female	☐ Male	**Sex:**	☐ Female	☐ Male

To be Completed by Interviewer This application was taken by:	Interviewer's Name (print or type) **JAMIE SUTTON**		Name and Address of Interviewer's Employer **ACME Lending Corp**
☐ Face-to-face interview ☐ Mail ☐ Telephone ☐ Internet	Interviewer's Signature	Date	123 Anywhere Your town, US (P) 111-234-5678 (F) 111-234-5677
	Interviewer's Phone Number (incl. area code) **555-555-5555**		

Continuation Sheet/Residential Loan Application

Use this continuation sheet if you need more space to complete the Residential Loan Application. Mark **B** for Borrower or **C** for Co-Borrower.	Borrower:	Agency Case Number:
	Co-Borrower:	Lender Case Number:

I/We fully understand that it is a Federal crime punishable by fine or imprisonment, or both, to knowingly make any false statements concerning any of the above facts as applicable under the provisions of Title 18, United States Code, Section 1001, et seq.

Borrower's Signature	Date	Co-Borrower's Signature	Date
X		X	

Section V. Monthly Income and Combined Housing Expense Information: The lender will use the income documents and W-2s provided for this calculation. Any supplemental earnings from sources other than employment are noted here as well. To the right of the income is a side-by-side comparison of housing expenses, both current and proposed. Note that taxes, insurance, mortgage insurance, and association dues are included in the proposed expense.

Section VI. Assets and Liabilities: The lender will compare the credit report with the information that you provide. Remember to include payments for child support and alimony here. Include cash as well as personal property values. The cash portion is verified through the banking and asset statements you provide. You will be asked to ballpark your personal property values as well as those for your automobiles. At the bottom of this section is a calculation of net worth, which is the difference between assets and liabilities. Hopefully this is a positive number. If you own any other real estate, this also is the place to list the property address and value/mortgage/rental income.

Section VII. Details of Transaction: A list of costs of the loan is a summary of the *Good Faith Estimate* (see Chapter 7). The sales price is added to the closing costs and prepaid expenses. The mortgage amount is subtracted, and the borrower's required cash to close is noted.

def•i•ni•tion

A lender is required by law to provide you with a written estimate of fees you will pay to get a loan. The **Good Faith Estimate of Closing Costs** is a disclosure offered by the lender within three days of a formal loan application that shows all fees associated with the purchase and any required impounds for escrow of taxes, insurance, or mortgage insurance.

Section VIII. Declarations: You will be asked to answer several questions. The material you provide to the lender will answer a lot of what he or she needs to know about you to determine your creditworthiness. However, the lender also will directly ask you about some other items. If you answer yes to any of these, other than those regarding U.S. citizenship, previous homeownership, and whether you intend to live in the home, you will be asked to explain. Your answers may affect your qualification. Because lending guides are so specific, your lender may learn something that would prompt him to redirect you to another loan solution.

Section IX. Acknowledgment and Agreement: Read the paragraph; if you agree to the terms, all parties sign.

It's Your Money

The practice of disclosure is not done to irritate the borrower, but rather to protect the borrower and future applicants. Loan applications are periodically audited by housing regulatory agencies to ensure that the lender is not "redlining," or selectively choosing to whom he or she will lend based upon race, gender, age, or other factors.

Section X. Information for Government Monitoring Purposes: This area of the application is set aside for borrower disclosure of race and sex. There are several race categories to choose from, and also an option to abstain. If you abstain from answering, the lender is still required to complete this portion to meet fair-lending criteria set forth by the federal government. Information about the interviewer and his or her phone number and address are also noted in this section.

Continuation Sheet/Residential Loan Application: Your application may have additional pages that are carry-over sections. In other words, not all of your information may fit into the sections available, so you may have to use an overflow section.

And of course, you must sign and date the bottom of the last page to indicate that the information you provided is accurate and true.

Underwriting

The final review of the application and all of its supporting documentation is called *underwriting*. This analysis determines to what extent the lender may be risking his assets. Every lender hopes that the monies lent to borrowers can be recovered through agreed-upon monthly payments over a predetermined period of time, or until the note is satisfied. Of course, things don't always go as anticipated. It's the underwriter's job to assess the risk, to the best of his or her ability, based upon a snapshot in time.

Underwriters are employees of the lender or individuals outside the company on contract, hired for the purpose of assessing risk on behalf of the lender.

Historically, underwriting has been done either by an individual or in a committee setting by a board that acts on behalf of the bank or lender.

def•i•ni•tion

> **Underwriting** is analyzing information to determine a borrower's ability to repay an obligation based upon credit, employment, and assets during a snapshot in time.

The underwriter reviews the paperwork and decides whether the client should receive the loan. The decision can be somewhat subjective, based upon the decision maker's previous experiences and resources. And it takes time and resources to review a file and all of its supporting documentation. Because it is not uncommon to wait 24 to 48 hours for a decision by an underwriter, only a few lenders still underwrite by this method on every file.

Instead, most lenders run file information directly through some type of automated underwriting (AU) system. Lenders have compiled statistical data on the performance of loans for decades, and this rich history tells them what characteristics make a good or bad loan. Credit, time on the job, and available assets all play a part in whether a loan is approved instantaneously by the automated underwriter or referred to an actual person for a final decision. The automated underwriting decision is usually completed in minutes. If the loan is approved, the file moves on to a loan processor, who checks that the income and asset information was typed in correctly.

If the automatic underwriting system refers the final decision to an underwriter, the loan package and all supporting documents are sent to the underwriter for review. One example of why a file may not pass through the automated process is if the proposed loan's ratios are too high for the program guidelines. An underwriter may look at the file and decide that in this situation it is okay to approve the loan because the borrower has more than enough money in the bank after the loan closes. Money left in the bank is considered a compensating factor and will offset the higher-than-normal ratios. It is the underwriter's job on all referred files to approve, deny, or provide a counteroffer to the borrower.

The preapproval process needs to be completed only once for the borrower, assuming that the outcome is what the buyer anticipated. Once approved, the borrower must purchase a home within a designated period of time, usually 90 days. The lender provides the borrower with a letter outlining the terms under which the approval is issued. The letter should stipulate that the loan is contingent upon the lender's inspection and approval of any home to be purchased. Remember, you as the borrower are only half of the equation of the approval. The other half is the home you decide to purchase.

Regulatory Disclosures and Disclaimers

Filling out form 1003 is only the beginning of the process a lender must follow to complete your loan application. The lending industry is highly regulated to protect the consumer against misrepresentation and fraud. Several regulatory disclosures and disclaimers are presented throughout the process, including the following documents (but keep in mind that this list may not include items particular to your state's laws):

- ◆ **Fair Housing Act.** This discloser indicating that a lender cannot refuse to make a loan application, provide different information, or refuse information to an applicant based upon race, color, national origin, religion, sex, marital status, or handicap.

- ◆ **Equal Credit Opportunity Act.** A disclosure indicating that a creditor must give equal consideration to an applicant, regardless of their gender, race, color, religion, national origin, sex, marital status, or age. This law granted women the right to purchase real estate with the same considerations as men.

- ◆ **Consumer Handbook for Adjustable Rate Mortgages** (ARM loans only). This outlines the ins and outs of ARM loans (for more information on ARM loans, see Chapter 9).

- ◆ **HUD Settlement Booklet** (FHA loans only). This is a complete guide to the loan application process, provided by the Department of Housing and Urban Development (HUD).

- ◆ **Home Mortgage Disclosure Act (HMDA).** This act was established to ensure lenders were meeting the lending needs of their community. If for whatever reason you do not complete the loan process, either because you withdraw the application or are denied a loan, you will receive a document confirming that you have not obtained a loan. Data about you and your demographics will then be added to the historical information already collected on cancelled loan files. Regulators watch closely to make certain there is no pattern to the loan cancellations based upon race, sex, or other discriminatory reasons.

◆ **Consumer Privacy Act (Gramm-Leach-Bliley Act).** As a borrower, you will be notified of your right to limit the distribution of your personal information amongst nonaffiliated third parties.

What Standards Must Be Met for an Underwriter?

Traditionally, underwriting decisions have been based on a borrower's housing-expenses-to-income relationship, or ratio, and the borrower's housing expense plus all other monthly obligations in relationship to income. As noted previously, in recent years the industry has moved away from this method of qualification, in favor of evaluating risks with computer-based automated underwriting systems. But for general purposes, the ratios are helpful in determining how much loan you can afford.

The following basic relationships are considered:

◆ Your housing expenses should not exceed 28 to 33 percent of your *gross monthly earnings.*

◆ Your housing expenses, in addition to all other long-term debt, should not exceed 36 to 41 percent of your gross monthly earnings.

def•i•ni•tion

Gross monthly earnings are defined as stable, predictable earnings. It's the amount your employer pays you before any taxes or withholdings are subtracted.

The 5 percent difference in the first two bullets (33–28 and 41–36) depends upon the loan type and the down payment on each loan product. When in doubt, hit the middle.

The lender's definition of housing expenses is principal, interest, taxes, and insurance, also abbreviated to *PITI.* The components are …

- **Principal and interest.** This calculation is the monthly amount the lender requires to repay the loan in the agreed amount of time.

- **Taxes.** One twelfth of annual property taxes are typically collected as part of the payment each month. Note that the lender requires evidence that all taxes are paid on the property, so that no tax agency can infringe on their first lien position.

It's Your Money

If you have 20 percent for a down payment, you may request to pay your own taxes and insurance rather than have the lender collect monthly (known as escrow). If you choose not to escrow, you can earn interest on your money and manage when the payments to the county and the insurance company are made. On the downside, taxes and insurance are typically required in lump-sum payments, so you may find it more comfortable to plan for them in the budget by allowing the lender to collect the amounts monthly.

- **Insurance.** One twelfth of the annual homeowner's insurance premium is required to be part of the payment the lender receives. Note that the lender requires, at a minimum, that fire insurance coverage be in place on the dwelling at all times. If the lender is ever notified of a lapse of insurance, the lender will immediately put a policy into place to cover the structure. The lender wants coverage to repair or replace the dwelling in case of damage caused by fire or the weather.

- **PMI/MIP.** This is a risk insurance known as private mortgage insurance (PMI) on conventional loans and mortgage insurance premium (MIP) on FHA loans.

These risk insurances are required by the lender to mitigate the risk on a loan to a borrower with less than a 20 percent down payment. This type of insurance is meant to offset the lender's exposure in case the borrower defaults on the loan and the lender has no choice but to pursue a foreclosure. In case of a foreclosure, a lender may recover only 70 to 75 percent of the original appraised value due to accrued interest, attorney fees, maintenance, and marketing costs. Lender's mortgage insurance offsets these expenses in the event of a claim. Lenders do not want you to walk away from your obligation of repayment because they would ultimately end up with the home, and they are not in the business of owning real estate.

◆ **Flood insurance.** If the home you want to purchase is located in a flood zone, you may be required to obtain flood insurance before the lender will finalize the loan. Your insurance provider can assist you in obtaining this government-guaranteed policy.

◆ **Homeowner's association dues.** These are fees associated with your housing development and are not paid to the lender. They are typically paid for maintenance and upkeep of common amenities, such as a pool or a clubhouse.

QUALIFICATION WORKSHEET

A. Gross Monthly Income   [   ] *

B. Housing Expense (Monthly)
    P & I
    Property taxes
    Homeowners Insurance
    PMI & MIP
    Total   [   ]

C. Recurring Debts (Monthly)
    Auto Payment(s)
    Student Loan(s)
    Revolving credit
    Child support received
    Alimony received
    other
    Total   [   ]

D. Total Monthly Debts (add B + C)   [   ]

E. Payment to Income Ratio (B÷A)   [   ] **

F. Total Debt to Income Ratio (D÷A)   [   ] ***

    *   calculated based upon hourly earnings or an average of previous two years.
    **   should not exceed 28% to 33%
    ***   should not exceed 36% to 40%

Use the sample qualification worksheet to determine your income-to-expenses ratio. Remember, the lender does not really use this calculation method for loan approval, but it may help you get an idea of what you could potentially qualify for.

Before You Sign _____

Contrary to popular belief, flooding is not covered as part of a typical homeowner's insurance policy. You may be covered if there is related wind or weather damage.

Most insurance carriers allow you to add policy riders to cover some aspects of flood damage. You would want a rider to cover you if, for example, your electricity went out during a storm, causing the sump pump to fail and your basement to flood.

As an example, let's say you earn $4,500 a month and you pay out monthly $569 in a car loan, student loan, and credit debt. The first ratio calculation, known as payment to income, is a relationship between your house payment ($1,176.75) divided by your gross monthly income ($4,500). The ratio is 26.15%. When you add your house payment to your other monthly obligations ($569) you get a total monthly debt of $1,745.75. Divide this number by your income of $4,500 for a ratio of 38.79%.

A. Gross Monthly Income   **$4,500.00***

B. Housing Expense (Monthly)

	P&I	$871.75
	Taxes	$200.00
	H.O. Ins.	$40.00
	PMI/MIP	$65.00
	Total	**$1,176.75**

C. Recurring Debts (Monthly)

	Auto	$320.00
	Student Loan	$125.00
	Credit Card	$45.00
	Personal Loan	$79.00
	Child Support	—
	Alimony	—
	Other	—
	Total	**$569.00**

D. Total Monthly Debts (B + C)   **$1,745.75**
E. Payment-to-Income Ratio (B ÷ A)   **26.15%****
F. Total Debt-to-Income Ratio (D ÷ A)   **38.79%*****

*Calculated based upon hourly earnings or an average of previous two years' earnings
**Should not exceed 28% to 33% ***Should not exceed 36% to 40%

Aside from the ratios, the underwriter looks for stability in employment, good credit, and any assets to close that are available and verifiable.

Keep in mind that this is not the way most loans are approved or denied today. This information is meant only as a guide. I stress this because if you do fall outside the ratios, it doesn't mean you're automatically disqualified. When your scenario is run through the lender's automated decision engine, it takes into account your circumstances and decides whether you are a satisfactory credit risk.

And what if, after careful consideration, both the computer and the underwriter do not approve your loan request? The lender is required to give you a detailed explanation of why he or she cannot grant you a loan. And if you're denied a loan because of your credit, you can request a free copy of the report.

Depending upon the reason, any of the following may be your next step:

♦ Postpone your purchase and take time to correct whatever may be the issue. For example, if you have too much debt, pay off a few things before you try again

♦ Talk to another lender. Not all lenders look at the same file the same way.

♦ Consider an alternative loan type. There may be another loan solution. Some lenders may not approve your first choice of loan program, but they may consider approval if you go a different route.

Explore all of these options. In some instances, it's better to wait and correct what needs to be corrected. Your interest rate, loan terms, and options likely will be better. If you do need to buy now, it's always worth continuing to look for other solutions. The next chapter tackles the question of what to do if you've been turned down for a loan or have circumstances that may present a problem for the lender.

The Least You Need to Know

◆ The loan application process can be done either on the phone, via e-mail, Internet, fax, or face to face. The standard form is relatively easy to complete, so be thorough. The more the lender knows up front the easier it is for them to give you accurate information about a loan.

◆ Today automated approval systems that have compiled historic statistical data make many underwriting decisions. Therefore, you cannot rely on the ratio method of qualification that has guided homebuyers for the last two decades.

◆ The loan application process provides you with disclosures that outline your rights as a homebuyer and consumer. The laws and acts have been put into place to limit discriminatory lending practices and give all potential borrowers equal access to the credit and homebuying process.

Chapter 5

Knowing Your Options If You Don't Fit the Mold

In This Chapter

- ◆ Finding out you're not the perfect customer for a mortgage
- ◆ Making do without the proper documents
- ◆ Reading a credit report
- ◆ Managing a poor credit rating

What happens if your calculation for a house payment exceeds what the lender believes you're capable of paying monthly? Or you don't have all of the paperwork necessary to properly document the file? Or your savings account balance hovers close to zero? What if your credit report has incorrect information, or shows slow pays on your credit cards from 10 years ago? Does that mean you can't get a mortgage loan? Absolutely not!

The preapproval process discussed in Chapters 3 and 4 is meant to pre-pare a potential homebuyer for a purchase in the near future. Many people discover after taking a good look at their finances that they need to do some work before they're ready to buy. This chapter offers a few suggestions on how to realign your financial profile to make you a more desirable client to a lender.

If you need to purchase a home right away and you don't have the time to rearrange your financial circumstances, you may need an alternative loan solution, which is the topic of Chapter 6. Either way, it's always better to know where you stand up front, before you have become emotionally involved with a potential home. There is nothing worse than falling in love with a new home and not being approved for a loan to purchase it.

Common Problems

Before considering the alternative solutions, let's work through common issues that may arise. Realize that there's a reason they call this an ap-proval *process*—it may take a few steps to get to the end result. Lenders are in the business of lending, and they will continue to evolve and de-velop loan programs to service their customers' needs. And they truly want to loan money to the right borrower with the right circumstances.

You Cannot Provide the Necessary Documentation

So what do you do if you don't have all of your income and asset infor-mation? In many cases, the lender can help you obtain copies of your paperwork. It's not uncommon for the lender to go directly to the source—let's say, your employer—and ask them to verify your position, income, and how long you've been on the job. The lender will need you to sign a consent form to authorize him or her to obtain informa-tion about you. Written requests are made all the time on behalf of borrowers; only in recent years have borrowers been encouraged to provide the information.

But what if you are unable to provide any documentation that will sub-stantiate your income or assets? You might find yourself in this situa-tion if, for example, you are a home day-care provider and your clients pay you by check every month. If you don't receive a regular pay stub, many lenders offer alternative means of verifying income. They've been known to use bank statements that show regular deposits to substantiate take-home pay. And there are the no-income and no-asset loans we introduced in Chapter 4.

You Don't Make Enough Money to Qualify

If you don't make enough money on your own to qualify for the mortgage, a co-mortgagor might help your cause. A co-mortgagor differs from a co-borrower in that this individual will not live in the property. This person's role is to boost the qualification of the borrower and offer another resource to the lender in case of default.

The co-mortgagor should be a parent, a relative, or someone you can substantiate a close relationship with. An adult child can also be a co-mortgagor for a parent. This individual(s) needs to be in good financial shape and be able to carry the extra monthly obligation.

The co-mortgagor will be asked to provide the same information that you have given. The co-mortgager's credit, income, and assets will be verified. He or she will sign all of the paperwork with the borrower and become jointly obligated for the repayment. The debt appears on both parties' credit reports, which may impact the co-mortgagor's debt ratios in the future.

The payment can be made by either borrower, but if the payment is split between each borrower, the interest deduction can be split. Good records need to be kept to show how much each party paid, but the co-mortgagor may receive a tax benefit for offering a helping hand. Check with a tax advisor for how to take advantage of this situation.

Certain restrictions apply, so rely on a lender to suggest when and if a co-mortgagor could improve your situation.

You Don't Have Much Money to Work With

Depending on how much time you have to prepare for the purchase, there are a couple of paths to follow if you're low on funds.

Cash will give you flexibility and a broader range of choices in how you finance your home. Having extra money in the bank is a great compensating factor for a lender if something else is off, such as ratios to qualify. Better rates also are given to borrowers with a down payment, not to mention that it's important to have a safety net in case you need a car repair or another kind of financial emergency arises. Here are a few ideas on how to improve your cash position:

- ◆ If you're disciplined, you may be in a position to save the money in your monthly budget, discussed in Chapter 1. A great deal of self-satisfaction arises from cutting the fat out of your spending and starting a savings plan. Consolidating your debt can also free up a few extra dollars each month.

- ◆ It's okay to accept gifts from a parent or relative. When word gets out you're buying a home, a few offers may be forthcoming. And if not, don't be too proud to ask. Many a homebuyer has been able to buy because of the generosity of another. And don't forget about the $10,000 gift clause in the IRS tax guides that could make it beneficial for the donor to give you the money. Check with a tax advisor for all of the pertinent details. If you do get a gift, the lender will need to document it.

> **It's Your Money**
>
> Don't hesitate to look for gift money from parents and relatives. If available, gifts can help to lighten the debt load for qualification.

- ◆ Convert an asset into cash. Sell a car that you own free and clear, or review your stock holdings and see if you might get a better rate of return if you sold them and bought a house. If you have a cash value on your insurance policy, now might be the time to take a loan against the money.

- ◆ Borrow against your 401(k). Each plan is different, but you may be able to borrow against the vested portion in the account. The loan is your money, and you pay yourself back—with interest!

- ◆ If you have an IRA, you are able to withdraw the money, without penalty, to purchase a home if you follow specific guidelines.

- ◆ If you're accustomed to receiving a tax refund, plan your home purchase in the spring and take advantage of the money Uncle Sam held for you all year.

If, after pursuing these options, you really cannot come up with any money, some loan options are still available. Many lenders and banks now offer lending solutions for the client with no money for a down payment. Chapter 10 covers a variety of ways to get into a home with little to no money from the borrower.

You Have Too Much Debt

Is it better to walk into the lender with no savings and no debt, or savings and debt? You have flexibility if you have the savings. If you have no debt but no savings, you've limited your options. Consider consolidating or paying off some of your balances after you have defined your loan direction. If you can improve your overall cash flow, reduce debt, and still keep a bit of money in your pocket, qualification may be easier.

In some cases, it makes sense to use your cash to pay off certain accounts outright. Say you've saved $10,000 and you owe $4,000 on credit cards, with required payments of $175 a month. A lender may advise you to pay off the credit card debit, which would still leave you with $6,000 in the bank. When you eliminate the monthly debt you're giving yourself that much more purchasing capacity.

If you don't have the up-front cash to wipe out your debts and you still need to trim your budget, put a plan into motion to pay minimum payments on all debts, but pay as much as you can on one. By paying off even one credit card, psychologically you're getting ahead of the interest game. After that debt is eliminated, take the extra cash and concentrate on the next obligation on your debt list. It's important in the beginning to choose a realistic liability—say, the card with the lowest balance. As you experience the success of eliminating debts, you can then choose to pay off other debts—for example, those with the highest interest rate. The key to this method is to focus on each debt individually rather than paying a little extra on all of your accounts.

Also check into consolidating a couple of accounts into one. When you condense the debt, more of the payment is likely to go toward paying off the balance than toward interest.

Credit Issues

If your credit report is less than perfect or reflects incorrect information, you'll need to resolve the problem. It is not uncommon to find something on a credit report that that has not been reported correctly, either because of mistaken identity or out of carelessness. And if there are derogatory items, such as late payments or collections, you'll need to be prepared to answer questions about them and explain the circumstances surrounding the account. Lenders scrutinize credit reports closely. How conscientious you've been with credit in the past is a direct indicator of how likely you are to repay a mortgage loan in the future.

Until the 1950s, most money lending was done within the community you lived in. Everyone knew each other, and a business transaction was sealed with a handshake. But as the credit card industry grew, lending services expanded across state lines and the need for accurate credit reporting was developed.

> **It's Your Money**
>
> Each of the three credit bureaus offers a wealth of information online and also allows you to request your free annual credit report through its website.

Your credit report is available to you, and I strongly recommend that you take the time to preview it for accuracy. In December 2003, a revision to the Fair Credit Reporting Act (you'll learn more about this act later in this chapter) required each of the three major credit bureaus to provide consumers with a copy of their credit report each year, free of charge. You can contact each of the credit bureaus directly for your free copy, either online, on the phone, or by mail.

Equifax
P.O. Box 740243
Atlanta, GA 30374
1-800-685-1111
www.equifax.com

Experian
P.O. Box 2002
Allen, TX 75013-3743
1-888-397-3742
www.experian.com

TransUnion
P.O. Box 1000
Chester, PA 19022
1-800-916-8800
www.transunion.com

The first time you see your own report, you may be astounded at how much about "you" is available to anyone who is authorized to look. By reviewing your own report, you will learn how the credit world perceives you. Your creditor provides data to the bureau, usually monthly. And it notes whether the account is current, whether the payment was received as agreed or late, and, if late, how late. Credit reports have a lot of specific details. There's no way to hide the fact if you don't make timely payments.

Collections are also reported to the bureau, along with contact information so you can resolve any disputes. A section of the report also is set aside for public-record information—evictions, legal disputes, a divorce, and tax liens all become part of your credit report.

Many reports provide individual account contacts as well. For example, if you have a Visa credit card, your report lists the address and phone number of the customer service office so you can contact it if you have a question about how your account was reported.

The report also indicates whether an account is open or closed. This information can be particularly useful for reconciling your report—we all have opened credit accounts for the fabulous one-time discount and then promptly forgotten about them. This is a great time to review what may still be open and close those accounts you don't use.

Your report is updated regularly. Each time you're billed by your creditors and you pay, they note the timeliness of your payment in their computers. Their computers then talk with the bureaus' computers, and your file reflects the new information. This sounds simple until you multiply by three bureaus, because all three need the information. And if your creditor doesn't report to all three bureaus, not all of the history is available. That's why it's a common practice for the lender to request a credit report that reflects information from all three bureaus, known as a tri-merge file.

If you find inaccurate information on your credit report, the lender typically will help you forward your dispute to the credit bureau who in turn sends it on to the creditor. The creditor is obliged to remove or correct any erroneous information within 30 days. The correction process can take some time, however, which is why it is a good idea to check your reports very early in your homebuying process.

Sample credit report.

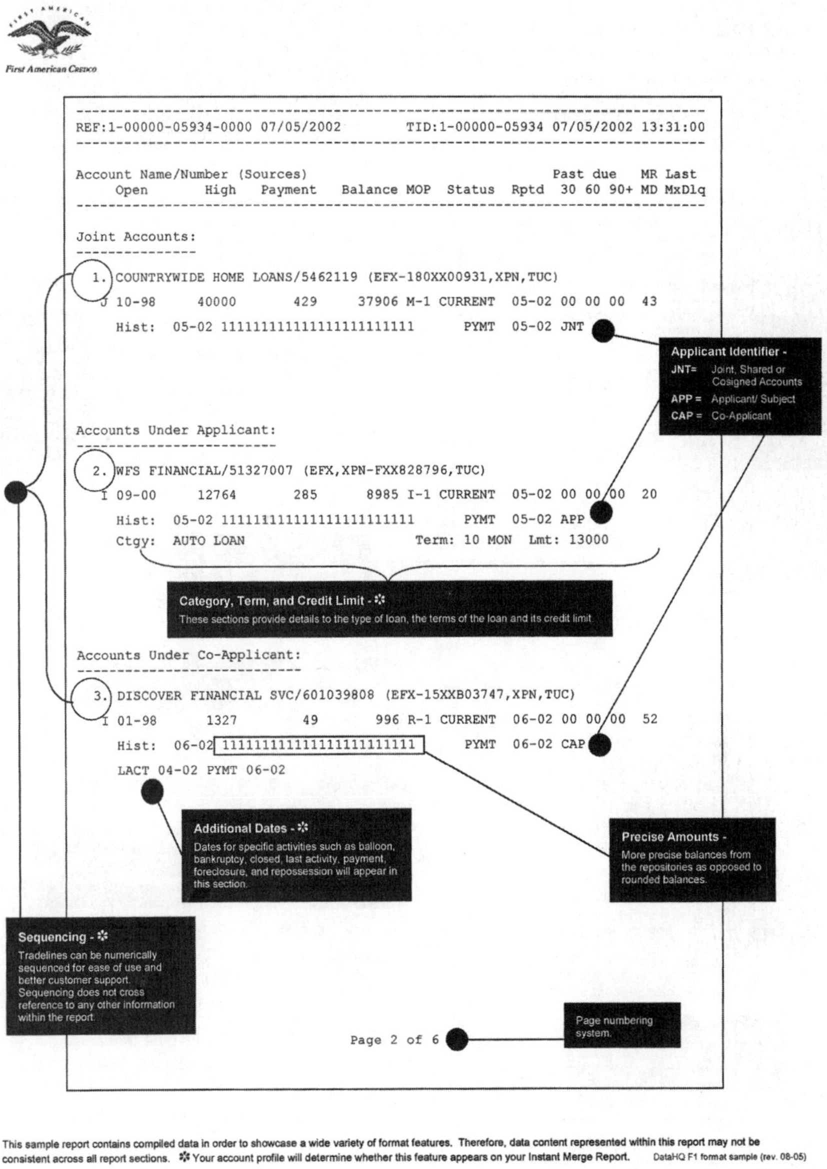
First American Credco

```
REF:1-00000-05934-0000 07/05/2002        TID:1-00000-05934 07/05/2002 13:31:00

Account Name/Number (Sources)                                 Past due    MR Last
     Open        High    Payment    Balance MOP  Status  Rptd  30 60 90+ MD MxDlq

Joint Accounts:

 1. COUNTRYWIDE HOME LOANS/5462119 (EFX-180XX00931,XPN,TUC)
   J 10-98      40000        429      37906 M-1 CURRENT  05-02 00 00 00  43
     Hist:  05-02 111111111111111111111111       PYMT   05-02 JNT

Accounts Under Applicant:

 2. WFS FINANCIAL/51327007 (EFX,XPN-FXX828796,TUC)
   I 09-00      12764        285       8985 I-1 CURRENT  05-02 00 00 00  20
     Hist:  05-02 111111111111111111111111       PYMT   05-02 APP
     Ctgy:  AUTO LOAN                     Term: 10 MON  Lmt: 13000

Accounts Under Co-Applicant:

 3. DISCOVER FINANCIAL SVC/601039808 (EFX-15XXB03747,XPN,TUC)
   I 01-98       1327         49        996 R-1 CURRENT  06-02 00 00 00  52
     Hist:  06-02 111111111111111111111111       PYMT   06-02 CAP
     LACT 04-02 PYMT 06-02

                                Page 2 of 6
```

Applicant Identifier -
JNT= Joint, Shared or Cosigned Accounts
APP = Applicant/ Subject
CAP = Co-Applicant

Category, Term, and Credit Limit - ✲
These sections provide details to the type of loan, the terms of the loan and its credit limit

Additional Dates - ✲
Dates for specific activities such as balloon, bankruptcy, closed, last activity, payment, foreclosure, and repossession will appear in this section.

Precise Amounts -
More precise balances from the repositories as opposed to rounded balances.

Sequencing - ✲
Tradelines can be numerically sequenced for ease of use and better customer support. Sequencing does not cross reference to any other information within the report.

Page numbering system.

This sample report contains compiled data in order to showcase a wide variety of format features. Therefore, data content represented within this report may not be consistent across all report sections. ✲ Your account profile will determine whether this feature appears on your Instant Merge Report. DataHQ F1 format sample (rev. 08-05)

First American Credco

```
------------------------------------------------------------------------
REF:1-00000-05934-0000 07/05/2002        TID:1-00000-05934 07/05/2002 13:31:00
------------------------------------------------------------------------

                    ****** DEROGATORY ITEMS ******

Account Name/Number (Sources)                        Past due   MR Last
    Open        High    Payment   Balance MOP Status Rptd 30 60 90+ MD MxDlq
------------------------------------------------------------------------

Joint Accounts:
---------------
BANK OF AMERICA MORTGA/1330469355684 (EFX*,XPN-FPXX86040*,TUC*)
    J 07-97    147286      1326    139339 M-2 DEL 30  06-02 09 01 00  59 06-02
      Hist:  06-02 2211112122121211121132211   PYMT  06-02 JNT      3 11-00
      Lates: 1x60:11-00 ; 9x30:6-02,5-02,12-01,10-01,9-01,6-01,2-01,10-00,9-00

CHEVRON U S A/734001 (EFX-906OC00024*,XPN*,TUC*)
    S 01-92     860        0             CLOSED R-5 DEL 120 05-02 01 02 01  98 05-02
      Hist:  05-02 543321111111111111111111    CLSD  05-02 JNT      5
      Lates: 2x90+:5-02,4-02 ; 2x60:3-02,2-02 ; 1x30:-1-02
      ACCT SUBMITTED TO COLLECTION; PAID COLL 05-02
      CREDIT CARD

GRANT & WEBER/G800CAL776113 (XPN-YC3980206*)
    I 01-98     230      N/A            130 Y-9 COLL/P&L 05-02 -  -  -   -
      Hist:  05-02 999                      PYMT  03-02 APP       9
      Lates:
      CN: CALIFORNIA PACIFIC
      ACCT SUBMITTED TO COLLECTION COLL 05-02

Accounts Under Applicant:
-------------------------
FNANB/CIRCUIT CITY/152300315866 (EFX-401HZ00615*,XPN*,TUC*)
    I 06-98    1186       33       742 R-1 CURRENT 06-02 02 01 03  48 05-01
      Hist:  06-02 1111111111111154325211111   PYMT  06-02 APP     5 05-01
      Lates: 3x90+:5-01,4-01,1-01 ; 1x60:3-01 ; 2x30:2-01,12-00
      REFER TO CONSUMER STATEMENT 1
      CREDIT CARD

Public Record Information:
--------------------------
Public Records may contain duplicate information. This report displays all
information reported by the repositories accessed.
   1. CH7 BANKRUPTCY FILED IN 02-98 JOINTLY; STATUS DISCHARGED 06-98; REPORTED
      02-98; FEDERAL DISTRICT COURT (LOS ANGELES, CA); DK: 9719582.
      (EFX-155VF00015,TUC) (JNT)

                    ****** END OF DEROGATORY ITEMS ******

                              Page 3 of 6
```

Lates - ✿
More detailed information on the late payments that have occurred with this tradeline.

Maximum Delinquency Section - ✿
Shows the maximum delinquency that occurred on this tradeline, information reported for up to seven years.

History Section -
Indicates month-to-month payment history pattern.

CN: Creditor Name -
More detailed creditor information for collection accounts.

Consumer Statement -
This notifies the customer that a consumer statement for this tradeline exists. See the **Consumer Statement** portion of this report for details.

Public Records Information -
When a public record does appear it will be accompanied by the subscriber code from the bureau reporting the data.

This sample report contains compiled data in order to showcase a wide variety of format features. Therefore, data content represented within this report may not be consistent across all report sections. ✿ Your account profile will determine whether this feature appears on your Instant Merge Report.   DataHQ F1 format sample (rev. 08-05)

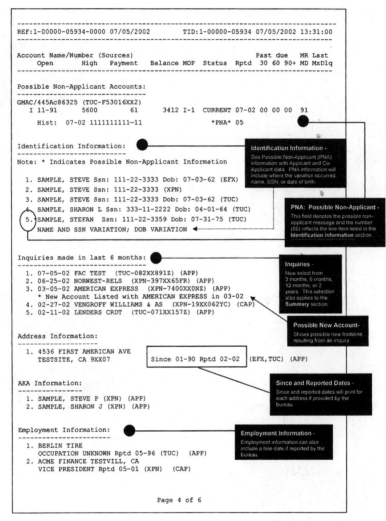

```
--------------------------------------------------------------------------
REF:1-00000-05934-0000 07/05/2002      TID:1-00000-05934 07/05/2002 13:31:00
--------------------------------------------------------------------------

Account Name/Number (Sources)                        Past due    MR Last
    Open         High    Payment    Balance MOP Status  Rptd 30 60 90+ MD MxDlq
--------------------------------------------------------------------------

Possible Non-Applicant Accounts:
---------------------------------
GMAC/445Ac86325 (TUC-F53016XX2)
    I 11-91      5600       61       3412 I-1  CURRENT 07-02 00 00 00  91

    Hist:   07-02 1111111111-11              *PNA* 05


Identification Information:
---------------------------
Note: * Indicates Possible Non-Applicant Information

   1. SAMPLE, STEVE Ssn: 111-22-3333 Dob: 07-03-62 (EFX)
   2. SAMPLE, STEVE Ssn: 111-22-3333 (XPN)
   3. SAMPLE, STEVE Ssn: 111-22-3333 Dob: 07-03-62 (TUC)
   4. SAMPLE, SHARON L Ssn: 333-11-2222 Dob: 04-01-64 (TUC)
   5. SAMPLE, STEFAN  Ssn: 111-22-3359 Dob: 07-31-75 (TUC)
      NAME AND SSN VARIATION; DOB VARIATION


Inquiries made in last 6 months:
--------------------------------
   1. 07-05-02 FAC TEST   (TUC-082XX891Z) (APP)
   2. 06-25-02 NORWEST-RELS  (XPN-397XX65FR) (APP)
   3. 03-05-02 AMERICAN EXPRESS  (XPN-7400XX0NZ) (APP)
      * New Account Listed with AMERICAN EXPRESS in 03-02
   4. 02-27-02 VENGROFF WILLIAMS & AS  (XPN-19XX062YC) (CAP)
   5. 02-11-02 LENDERS CRDT  (TUC-071XX157Z) (APP)

Address Information:
--------------------
   1. 4536 FIRST AMERICAN AVE
      TESTSITE, CA 9XX07        Since 01-90 Rptd 02-02  (EFX,TUC) (APP)


AKA Information:
----------------
   1. SAMPLE, STEVE P (XPN) (APP)
   2. SAMPLE, SHARON J (XPN) (APP)


Employment Information:
-----------------------
   1. BERLIN TIRE
      OCCUPATION UNKNOWN Rptd 05-96 (TUC)   (APP)
   2. ACME FINANCE TESTVILL, CA
      VICE PRESIDENT Rptd 05-01 (XPN)  (CAP)



                        Page 4 of 6
```

Identification Information -
See Possible Non-Applicant (PNA) information with Applicant and Co-Applicant data. PNA information will include where the variation occurred, name, SSN, or date of birth.

PNA: Possible Non-Applicant -
This field denotes the possible non-applicant message and the number (05) reflects the line item listed in the **Identification Information** section.

Inquiries -
Now select from 3 months, 6 months, 12 months, or 2 years. This selection also applies to the **Summary** section.

Possible New Account-
Shows possible new tradeline resulting from an inquiry.

Since and Reported Dates -
Since and reported dates will print for each address if provided by the bureau.

Employment Information -
Employment information can also include a hire date if reported by the bureau.

First American Credco

```
--------------------------------------------------------------------------------
REF:1-00000-05934-0000 07/05/2002       TID:1-00000-05934 07/05/2002 13:31:00
--------------------------------------------------------------------------------

Miscellaneous Information:
-------------------------
  1. Consumer has Active Duty Alert. (XPN) (CAP)
  2. Consumer has Initial Fraud Alert. (TUC) (CAP)
  3. Variation between Inquiry and Onfile address. (TUC) (CAP)

Consumer Statement:
-------------------
  1. ACTIVE DUTY ALERT. CONSUMER HAS REQUESTED AN ALERT BE PLACED ON THEIR
     CREDIT FILE. 123 EAGLE ROAD, TOMORROW, OR 99500 DAYTIME 7709991212
     EVENING 7708883434 Rptd 02-05 (EFX)(APP)
  2. FRAUD VICTIM. "EXTENDED ALERT". CONSUMER HAS REQUESTED AN ALERT BE PLACED
     ON THEIR CREDIT FILE. PAGER 7704445555. Rptd 03-05 (EFX)(CAP)
  3. ACCOUNT WENT TO A DELINQUENT STATUS WHILE I WAS OUT OF THE COUNTRY.
     Rptd 05-05 (XPN)(CAP)
  4. 26& 04-22-05 000000 ID SECURITY ALERT: FRAUDLENT APPLICATIONS MAY BE
     SUBMITTED IN MY NAME OR MY IDENTITY MAY HAVE BEEN USED WITHOUT MY CONSENT
     TO FRAUDULENTLY OBTAIN GOODS OR SERVICES. THIS ALERT WILL BE MAINTAINED
     ON FILE FOR 90 DAYS BEGINNING 05/22/05. Rptd 04/05 (XPN)(APP)
  5. #HK#IFCRA-INITIAL FRAUD ALERT: ACTION MAY BE REQUIRED UNDER FCRA BEFORE
     OPENING OR MODIFYING AN ACCOUNT.  CONTACT CONSUMER AT (312)555-1212
     Rptd 04-05 (TUC)(APP)
  6. #HK# ID FRAUD VICTIM ALERT. FRAUDULENT APPLICATION MAY BE SUBMITTED IN MY
     NAME USING CORRECT PERSONAL INFORMATION.  DO NOT EXTEND CREDIT WITHOUT
     FIRST CONTACTING ME PERSONALLY AND VERIFYING ALL APPLICANT INFORMATION.
     CONTACT CONSUMER AT (312)555-1212 Rptd 04-05 (TUC)(APP)
  7. MY PAYCHECK WAS DELAYED BY 6 WEEKS AND THEREFORE I COULD NOT PAY THE GAS
     CARD ON TIME. Rptd 05-05 (TUC)(CAP)


Decode Directory Information:
-----------------------------
  1. A F S C I (XPN-3564330)
     (310)370-4854 17508 HAWTHORNE BLVD TORRANCE CA 90504
  2. A F S C I (TUC-086XX30FR)
     (800)377-4800 17508 HAWTHORNE BOULEVARD TORRANCE CA 90504

Fraud Verification Information:
-------------------------------
  EFX SAFESCAN (APP)
     SAFESCANNED: YOUR INQUIRY HAS GONE THROUGH
     OUR SAFESCAN DATA BASE; SSN ISSUED 1969 IN HI.
  EFX SAFESCAN (CAP)
     Not provided by the repository.
  EFX SAFESCAN (PNA)
     SUB-SEGMENT DATA ONLY; SINCE 11-07-2000 THE SSN HAS BEEN USED
     3 TIMES IN OTHER INQUIRIES;
  TUC HRFA (APP)
     AVAILABLE AND CLEAR
  TUC HRFA (CAP)
     Match not found

                              Page 5 of 6
```

Alert details –
FACT Act Alert specific details will be displayed in either the Miscellaneous Information or the Consumer Statement section depending on the bureau. Consumer statement details may vary by the consumer and the reporting bureau.

Decode Directory Information - ❊
The creditor information will now include the bureau-specific subscriber code and a phone number, when available. These decode products from the bureaus are available: Direct Check, Creditor Contact Info and On Line Directory.

Fraud Verification Information - ❊
When a fraud message does appear it will show whom the message pertains to: APP, CAP or PNA. Fraud products available from the bureaus include HRFA, Fraud Shield, and Safescan.

This sample report contains compiled data in order to showcase a wide variety of format features. Therefore, data content represented within this report may not be consistent across all report sections. ❊ Your account profile will determine whether this feature appears on your Instant Merge Report. DataHQ F1 format sample (rev. 08-05)

First American Credco

```
--------------------------------------------------------------------------------
REF:1-00000-05934-0000 07/05/2002       TID:1-00000-05934 07/05/2002 13:31:00
--------------------------------------------------------------------------------

Consumer Referral Information:
------------------------------
  EFX - EQUIFAX INFORMATION SVCS, PHONE: (800) 685-1111
        P.O. BOX 740241, ATLANTA, GA 30374
  XPN - EXPERIAN, PHONE: (888) 397-3742
        P.O. BOX 2002, ALLEN, TX 75013
  TUC - TRANSUNION, PHONE: (800) 888-4213
        2 BALDWIN PLACE, PO BOX 1000, CHESTER, PA 19022

Error Information:        ●
------------------
  1. TUC DATA UNAVAILABLE.  (TUC-E021, TUC-E160)


Prepared By:   First American CREDCO
               12395 First American Way, Suite 200
               Poway, CA 92064-0495
               Contact Phone: (800)300-3032    Fax:(800) 938-7200
```

Error Information - ✿

If there are any issues with processing this report, special messages regarding the state of the file will appear in this section. It will include a generic text message (i.e., applicant file frozen, possible incomplete data, etc.), as well as corresponding specific error codes (i.e., missing information, invalid subscriber code, etc.)

This report contains information supplied by the repositories named above. Its contents have not been verified by First American CREDCO and may contain duplicate information. While this report is being used for some real estate lending purposes, it is not a Residential Mortgage Credit Report as defined by FNMA, FHLMC, and FHA/VA guidelines.

```
                   ****** END OF INSTANT MERGE REPORT ******
```

This sample report contains compiled data in order to showcase a wide variety of format features. Therefore, data content represented within this report may not be consistent across all report sections. ✿ Your account profile will determine whether this feature appears on your Instant Merge Report.   DataHQ F1 format sample (rev. 08-05)

Instant Merge® Sample Report
Tradeline Key

```
--------------------------------------------------------------------------------
Account Name/Number (Sources)                              Past due    MR   Last
   Open      High   Payment Balance MOP   Status   Rptd   30  60  90+  MD   MxDlq
--------------------------------------------------------------------------------
                                            1
   BANK OF AMERICA MORTGA/1003075352461 (EFX* XPN-FPXX86040*, TUC*)

 2                      3      4     5               6            7          8    9
 J  07-97  147286     1326  139339 M-2   DEL 30    06-02   07  02  06   59   06-02
                                                                 11        12   13
10 Hist:  06-02 221166554432211121132211   PYMT    06-02         JNT       6    02-02

14 Ctgy:  REAL ESTATE                        Term:  30 YRS           Lmt:  147,000

15 Lates: 6x90+:2-02,1-02,12-01,11-01,10-01,9-01; 2x60:8-01,11-00; 7x30:6-02,ADDTNL LATES

16 BLON 04-00 LACT 06-02 PYMT 06-02
```

1 The SOURCES for each tradeline, with the subscriber code provided from the most recently reported repository. An asterisk (*) indicates which repository reported derogatory information. EFX = Equifax; XPN = Experian; TUC = TransUnion.

2 ECOA code indicates who is responsible for each account and the type of participation for that account, as follows:

U	UNDESIGNATED	Not designated by the creditor
I	INDIVIDUAL	Individual account
J	JOINT	Joint account
A	AUTHORIZED USER	Authorized to use someone else's account
S	SHARED	Joint account
C	CO-MAKER	Joint responsibility for the account
B	CO-SIGNER	Responsibility only in case of default on the account
M	MAKER	Individual account
T	TERMINATED	Closed account
X	DECEASED	Deceased individual

3 PYMT displays the monthly liability on each account.

4 BALANCE displays the total liability on each account.

5 MOP *(Method of Payment)* and STATUS use the "Universal Rating Code" with English translation of the current status of the account as of the date reported.

MOP Codes

Account type:

R	Revolving	O	Open, 30 days	C	Line of Credit
I	Installment	M	Mortgage	Y	External Collection

Universal Rating Code:		English Translation:
0	Too new to rate	CURRENT
1	Current	CURRENT
2	30 days late	DEL 30
3	60 days late	DEL 60
4	90 days late	DEL 90
5	120 days late	DEL 120
6	150 days late	DEL 150
7	Wage Earner Plan or Bankruptcy	WEP/BKRP
8	Repossession or Foreclosure	REPO/FCL
9	Collection or Charge-off	COLL/P&L
U	Unrated	UNRATED

6 RPTD displays the date the account was reported by the creditor.

7 PAST DUE displays the number of times the account has been 30, 60, or 90+ days past due within the last seven years.

8 MR *(Months Reviewed)* is the number of months of payment history reported by the repositories.

9 LAST DLQ displays the date of the most recent delinquency, if reported by the creditor.

10 HIST *(Historical Payment Pattern)* indicates month to month payment history with the most recent date reported at the left. If reported, displays up to the last 24 months. For numbers other than 1, refer to "Universal Rating Code." A dash (-) means not reported that month.

11 Applicant Identifier. Identifies the owner of an account by (JNT) joint, (APP) applicant/subject, (CAP) co-applicant, or (*PNA*) possible non-applicant.

12 MD *(Maximum Delinquency)* displays the most severe delinquency for the account by MOP code up to 6.

13 MAX DLQ *(Maximum Delinquency Date)* displays the date of the most severe delinquency.

14 CTGY, TERM, LMT displays the category of loan, the terms of the loan and its credit limit.

15 LATES displays more detailed information on the late payments that have occurred with this tradeline.

16 ADDITIONAL DATES and amounts posted for specific categories like balloon, bankruptcy, closed, last activity, payment, foreclosure, and repossession.

This sample report contains compiled data in order to showcase a wide variety of format features. Therefore, data content represented within this report may not be consistent across all report sections. ✿ Your account profile will determine whether this feature appears on your Instant Merge Report.   DataHQ F1 Format Sample Key (rev. 07-05)

It's Your Money _____

Credit fraud and identity theft happen all too frequently. Often you can prevent misuse of your information by being aware of how you allow your credit data to be used. Take time to consider how many available credit cards you have in your name, and consider closing those you don't use. Also be cautious in giving out your personal information, particularly when dealing with phone solicitors and when making Internet purchases.

Understanding Your Credit Score

Since the inception of credit reporting in the 1950s, companies have been keeping tabs on their clients' spending and repayment patterns. Today the data is all gathered electronically and all types of credit performance is rated according to a model developed by Fair, Isaac and Company.

The credit score takes into account the amount of open and available credit, how much outstanding debt you have, and how much may be available to you. The statistics also track how well you pay your monthly obligations, how long you've had credit, and how recently you have taken on new debt. Your mix of installment versus revolving debt also influences the score. Each bureau has a slightly different idea of which of these characteristics is the most important, so your score is likely to be different with each bureau.

It's Your Money _____

If you and a spouse or partner have joint loans and credit cards, your scores are independent of one another. The mortgage lender will choose the middle score as a guide; if there is more than one borrower, the lender will choose the lowest middle score of the two.

Scores range from 300 to 900, with 900 being a superior rating. I've never seen a score greater 820, so it's fair to say that a score in the mid-700 range and up is excellent.

The credit score is important to you for these reasons:

◆ Many loan institutions offer abbreviated underwriting standards for credit scores above 720.

♦ If your credit score is below 620, subprime lending standards kick in. Depending on how quickly you need to borrow, there may be time to improve it!

♦ Lenders offer their loan programs and rates based upon credit scores with the thought that they'll extend the best rates to the best clients.

When you receive your credit score, determine what is influencing it. Common reasons why a score may not be as high as you'd like include late payments, outstanding collections, high outstanding credit limits on revolving cards, and serious credit disturbances such as judgments, tax liens, or bankruptcy.

In some cases, a single account may have gone undetected for an extended period of time. For example, you may have an old phone bill from your first apartment many years ago that has gone unpaid, and it may never have been brought to your attention until now. Or your credit may not be mature enough to rebound on its own. Remember, the credit-scoring process reviews your history, and, as time passes and good credit is re-established, the averaging process raises your score.

The credit score can be influenced by the number of times a credit report is reviewed, so it's a good practice to limit the amount of exposure to your credit. Particularly harmful are a few trips to various car dealerships, where salespeople try to be helpful and find the best financing solution for that sporty new car. Each creditor typically wants to look at his or her own version of credit, and it's easy to rack up four or five pulls within a 24-hour period.

It's said that when multiple pulls are made in a short period of time to allow a client to explore financing options for a home or auto purchase, the score should not be impacted. But the computer notes the inquiries as a new concentrated spur of activity, and that kind of activity could be treated as derogatory. If that does occur, your credit score will be ratcheted downward. In other words, there is no guarantee that your credit score will not be affected.

When you've determined what's on your report, immediately take steps to correct problems. If you're behind on your credit card, be proactive and make arrangements with the creditor. Although it's an unpleasant call to make, they are more likely to work with you if you contact them than if you wait for them to contact you.

Your credit report is updated regularly, so by taking measures toward improving your credit position, you are taking a step toward improving your score over time. When you pay a debt, the payment is reported to the credit bureaus; over a 60- to 90-day period, it will be reflected on your credit report.

If you're in a hurry and cannot wait for the score to naturally increase over the next three to six months, a rescore procedure is available. Suppose that for the past several years you have had an outstanding collection of $1,000, and you paid it off today. It was noted on your report by all three bureaus, and we'll assume it has affected your score. A slightly higher score would help you get into a better loan program. Rather than wait for the creditor to report the payment, the reporting company that the lender used to request the credit report can initiate a process whereby each bureau is notified of the collection payoff immediately. Each bureau is asked to update the information as soon as possible and again run the automated system to rescore the client's credit.

This procedure can be costly. A credit-reporting company can charge $30 to $50 per account, per bureau, for the rush, and there is no guarantee that the new score will be what you wanted or expected.

Tips for Increasing Your Credit Score

No exact information is available for increasing your score because the mathematical formula established by Fair, Isaac and Company is kept secret to prevent credit manipulation. However, here are a few suggestions:

- ♦ Reduce your available credit. Close out unwanted and unused credit cards so that on paper you cannot borrow as much.

- ♦ Don't overdo credit usage. A mortgage is okay; a lot of revolving credit is not.

- ♦ Extend yourself only up to 50 percent of your available limit on a credit card. If your limit is $5,000, never allow your balance to exceed $2,500.

- Keep credit inquiries to a minimum. Let someone check your credit only if absolutely necessary.

- Never go over your credit limit.

- Pay your obligations on time. If this has been a problem in the past, establish an automatic withdrawal payment plan through your creditor to ensure payment as agreed.

- Have old, old debt evaluated before you pay it off. Suppose you have an old utility bill in collection status from college six years ago. By reopening the debt to pay it off, you are, in effect, adding a new derogatory entry to your credit file, and it could actually drop your score for a period of time. It might be wise to hold off on paying it.

Correcting Your Report

When you review your credit report, be alert to discrepancies and mis-information. With the vast amount of data that's transmitted on a daily basis, it's a wonder more errors aren't made!

Credit histories do get crossed occasionally. As you would expect, criss-crossed credit appears in families with Jr.'s or Sr.'s, or for folks with regular names such as James Smith. When a lender pulls your credit report, he or she reviews the report to see if it matches up with information the borrower has provided. And the new guidelines for the Fair Credit Reporting Act (FCRA) state that if it doesn't match up, the lender will need to determine why. Expect the lender to request your help to correct erroneous entries.

def•i•ni•tion

The **Fair Credit Reporting Act** is legislation stating that borrowers have the right to a free copy of their report if they are denied credit, with assistance to correct invalid information.

If you discover incorrect information on your credit report that may negatively influence your score, you may dispute the information and ask for a correction. Under the guides of the *Fair Credit Reporting Act*, if you dispute an account and send a letter, the reporting bureau is permitted 30 days to investigate and correct erroneous information. The entry must be removed if it cannot be shown the account is valid. After the information has been corrected, a new credit score can be obtained. Note that each of the three credit bureaus must be contacted to ensure that the information is properly distributed in your credit history.

Divorce tends to muddy a credit report. It's not unusual for a spouse's credit information to appear on the other spouse's report. But when the client is divorced and debt appears on the account that is in both names, you must provide the lender with a divorce decree to explain who is responsible for the debt. The mortgage lender will qualify the borrower only with debts that are part of the borrower's obligation as stated by the courts, as long as they've been paid as agreed and have a satisfactory rating.

Something not all divorce attorneys will tell you, though, is how important it is that you close out all joint accounts. Even though the mortgage lender will abide by the divorce decree when looking at debts, a creditor may never release you from your obligation until the account has been closed out. I've seen more than one ugly credit report where the disgruntled ex-spouse has set out to sabotage the other's credit by refusing to pay or by filing bankruptcy to get out from underneath the joint debt. In such a case, you are left holding the bag, even if your remaining credit is spotless.

If You Have No Credit

Some people haven't established traditional credit usage, such as installment loans or credit cards. Yet a large part of the mortgage underwriter's decision lies with the borrower's ability to pay his or her monthly obligations. And some loan programs require a minimum of three or four active trade lines (entries from creditors) on a report before even considering lending money to someone. If a credit report is pulled and there are no trade lines, not enough trade lines exist, or the credit is not seasoned (less than two years old), an alternative credit report can be created.

Typically, credit card companies and loan institutions report regularly to the credit bureaus. But in the case of someone who doesn't have cards and loans, rent verification from a landlord, or utility payments for gas, electric, and telephone can be added.

The borrower should contact anyone regular payments have been made to—even a doctor, dentist, or hospital. Call the company and ask for a payment-history letter. The letter should state the client's name, the type of account, and the payment history or quality of payment (such as "Paid as agreed"). The lender can provide the data to the credit bureau on behalf of the borrower, and a credit report will be created. It's not possible, however, to obtain a credit score with a nontraditional credit report, so some types of financing may not be available.

> **It's Your Money**
>
> Loans provided through the Federal Housing Administration (FHA) have no minimum credit score requirements, and the guidelines state that a borrower cannot be denied for lack of credit.

Resolving Poor Credit

As we've established, credit is a big part of the loan-approval process, and if debt is not paid as agreed, credit ratings drop. One or two slow pays typically require a brief explanation. But as more payments are missed, your overall credit becomes tarnished. To obtain a loan with the best interest rates, debts should be paid as agreed for a minimum of 12 to 18 months.

If you know you have a credit problem, address it now because the issue will not disappear on its own. The longer an account remains unresolved, the more of a hassle it might become. The account may be transferred between different entities, and it becomes more difficult to settle as time goes on. Most creditors want a resolution. They are willing to negotiate the terms with you, and sometimes that means settling for less than the total amount.

> **It's Your Money**
>
> Each credit-reporting service has its own name for its score: TransUnion calls its score empirica, Experian uses fair isaac or fico, and Equifax is known as a beacon score. These scores, or numbers, are what an underwriter uses to help make a determination on your creditworthiness.

Your lender should be able to offer suggestions for how to resolve any credit problems. I cannot tell you how many times I've met with a client who has said they know there's something there but they don't know how serious it is. Be prepared to tackle the demon and get past it. After all, you're not the first, nor will you be the last, to have a few bruises appear on your credit. The great news is that credit issues can be resolved and tucked away as only a memory. And a lot of the time, they're not as bad as you think.

Bankruptcy

A bankruptcy suggests serious credit problems. Two types of personal bankruptcy exist:

♦ **Chapter 7.** All debt is written off. The creditors are notified, and the courts forgive the obligations 100 percent. Federal laws enacted in 2005 make it more difficult to declare Chapter 7 bankruptcy.

♦ **Chapter 13.** Debt is repaid on a schedule set up through a court-appointed trustee. The creditors are asked to take an abbreviated settlement, but the client agrees to pay back a large portion of the indebtedness over a two- to five-year period. A consolidated payment is made to the trustee, who, in turn, disperses the monies to the creditors on a monthly basis.

Your conscience and your attorney will help you to decide which is best for you. The lender would prefer to see that you've filed the Chapter 13, which shows you have honored, at least in part, the obligations to your creditors. That doesn't forgive you for the credit mishap, but it does show your intent to correct the problem.

For conforming loans, the bankruptcy needs to have been settled, or discharged, a minimum of three to five years ago, depending on loan type. There are exceptions to every rule in financing, it seems. In this case, *if* the bankruptcy was the result of a catastrophic event, such as the death of the primary wage earner, or insurmountable medical debt due to illness, the waiting period may be shortened.

Also, the borrower must be able to show that credit has been re-established. New credit needs to be paid as agreed. So don't let yourself avoid credit after a bankruptcy. Embrace the bankruptcy as a learning experience, and apply for a secured loan or a debit card tied to a bank account. You're not encouraged to go back into debt, but rather to show that you are capable of repaying an obligation in a timely fashion. If you find yourself in this situation, the next time you need new tires for your car, try to establish a 90-days-same-as-cash account and pay it off in the timeline agreed. If you cannot get the loan in your own name, seek out a co-signer to help you get back on your feet.

Although bankruptcy is a serious credit concern, it need not be considered an insurmountable obstacle when borrowing. There are guidelines in place to help you buy eventually. If you can't wait for your credit to improve, the subprime lending industry has evolved to meet this demand. You may be eligible for a loan, but the rate will be higher. Consider the opportunity if you can agree on the payment and terms. These loans can also help you quickly re-establish credit. Nothing says that, in a year or two, you won't be back on your feet and ready to refinance to a lower interest rate–conforming loan. Chapter 13 is devoted to refinancing.

Credit Counseling

Many consumers have turned to credit-counseling companies for guidance when trying to handle their debt. Credit counselors serve one goal at two different stages: money management before and after clients get in over their heads. Some of these services have changed the lives of consumers in a very positive way.

Good counselors and legitimate companies help establish budgets and educate clients on money management. Many also have programs in place in which you make a lump-sum payment to the service, and they, in turn, distribute it among your creditors (for a fee) so that you avoid getting in over your head. If you're having problems paying your debts but are still making regular payments, the service may even be able to negotiate a settlement, based upon a guaranteed payback, before your credit deteriorates. In this case, the lender views the service as a proactive attempt at maintaining good credit.

Credit counselors also help clients whose debt is spinning out of control because of excessive credit obligations. In this case, they are helping the client avoid bankruptcy. The service negotiates on the client's behalf to reduce the balances owed and acts as the payment clearing-house. The client makes a payment to the service, and the service distributes money to the creditors (again, for a fee). The creditor will usually note on the credit report that the client is participating in credit counseling.

It's important to understand how a mortgage lender views these two separate examples. If you have contracted with a credit counselor because you're trying to be proactive and "manage" your money, and your payment history is good, then the mortgage lender will likely look favorably on the service. If you've entered into the plan out of financial duress, then the lender may ask for a letter from the plan administrator indicating that they know you're contemplating a home purchase and that they give their approval. Usually, the letter must state that you've participated in the program for a minimum of 12 months and are able to handle a new obligation.

If you were having difficulty paying your debts and contracted with one of these organizations, the process is viewed more like a bankruptcy, whereby you may be required to pay off the balance of the loan and wait a period of time to purchase.

From the lender's viewpoint, if you felt the need to contact and contract with this type of organization, your credit position warrants a let's-wait-and-see attitude, hence at least 12 months. And although you were proactive in your money management and have avoided bankruptcy proceedings, it may still influence your lender's decision and loan program.

Before You Sign

Not all credit-counseling companies have the consumer's best interests at heart. Many "counselors" are, in fact, salesmen and saleswomen representing debt-consolidation companies, selling a high-interest-rate loan. Some companies make claims such as their ability to remove all derogatory credit legitimately. You might worry about a company that feels the need to tell you they are legitimate. Ask for references and consult with your own creditors to see if they have worked well with them in the past.

The Least You Need to Know

- It's okay to have circumstances outside of the box; there are still financing solutions available.

- Be proactive when it comes to your credit. Request a report, review its content, and get busy to correct any items that either are not correct or have a negative impact on your credit well-being.

- Your credit score is influenced by the amount of credit and the combination of installment and revolving accounts, as well as how timely you are at repayment.

- Credit counseling is an option for both the client with great credit that needs some guidance and the client who has lost control of credit and needs help pulling it back together. Be cautious when choosing the counselor, and understand the counselor's agenda before entrusting him or her with your history.

Chapter 6

Alternative Lending: Subprime Mortgages

In This Chapter

- ◆ Learning about the subprime lending market
- ◆ Applying for a subprime loan
- ◆ Becoming aware of predatory lending practices
- ◆ Protecting yourself against predatory lending

Even if your credit circumstances cannot be resolved or you cannot produce the necessary documentation to move forward on the traditional mortgage loan, you may still be able to obtain financing. An entire lending practice exists to offer loans that don't fit the traditional mold.

Alternative Solution Financing

The mortgage industry is proactive when it comes to creating lending solutions that meet consumer needs. When a need repeatedly arises—for a lower-cost loan, for instance—the lending community comes together with an *alternative* loan solution to match the need. We've already touched on a few alternatives up to this point in the book, including reduced-doc and no-doc loans, discussed in Chapter 3.

def•i•ni•tion _____

Subprime refers to loans that are outside the prime, or standard, lending arena.

As debt in our society has risen, so has the incidence of slow payments among credit users. And traditional lending guidelines had no place for a loan that had below-standard credit circumstances. So the industry stepped up with an alternative, known as the *subprime* lending market.

Understanding Prime and Subprime Loans

The mortgage industry historically has set high standards for buyers. To get a prime loan, also known as an *A paper loan*, borrowers generally must have good credit and verifiable income and assets. Borrowers who fall into this category can expect the best terms and lowest interest rates, and by far the most options when it comes to choosing a lending institution. Lenders are very eager to provide money to these buyers.

def•i•ni•tion _____

Credit is rated, with **A** being the best, **A–** being a few credit slips, and **B/C** credit showing several late payments, derogatory creditor comments, and perhaps even collections and bankruptcy. As your credit slips from perfect, the interest rates rise, as much as several percentage points higher than for perfect credit.

A loan for someone with excellent credit is known as an **A paper loan.**

Lenders knew that their stringent lending requirements kept away a large potential client base. And they knew that if they accepted a bit more risk, they could make more loans and thus more money. Hence, industry expectations have changed dramatically in the last 20 years, and it's almost as if two lending practices evolved out of one.

Loans that don't meet traditional standards and that have significant credit irregularities are categorized today as *B/C* loans. B/C loans generally have a credit score below 620. Characteristics include derogatory credit, such as slow payments or late payments, bankruptcy, foreclosure, tax liens, repossessions, collections, and judgments. Any loan that may require a different type of documentation and may or may not have a low credit score could also find a home in the B/C category. For example, if there no record of income, such as for a restaurant server who receives tip income but does not report 100 percent of the income, a *B/C* loan might be necessary.

It's Your Money

It is estimated that more than 80 percent of potential homebuyers have some type of blemish on their credit report. Don't assume that because you've had a few late payments or have even filed bankruptcy in the past that you must use a subprime loan. There is a very gray line between prime/subprime loan guidelines. Always approach the application process as if you are an *A* paper loan and let the lender tell you otherwise. A lender will identify the options for you and suggest the *B/C* alternative only if necessary.

Not every lender offers subprime loans. If they don't offer them in-house, your loan officer will likely refer you to a lender who does. It has become such a big part of the industry that lenders cannot do their jobs effectively without a subprime resource.

Expect the subprime loan to be a bit more expensive. For example, a loan that fits the model for a *conforming* loan may be offered at a 6 percent interest rate, while a subprime loan might warrant an 8 percent interest rate. In other words, expect to pay more for the underwriting exception, just as you would if you were to order a one-of-a-kind, tailor-made suit. When you require a custom product, you pay extra for that service.

def·i·ni·tion

Conforming refers to loans that meet the standards set forth by the lending community.

Even though you are using an alternative loan type, you should still shop for the best possible financing package—even if you've been referred to the lender. Compare a couple of companies, their rates, and the programs that may be available. Each lender looks at the risk a bit differently, and the charge for that interest rate will vary depending upon how severe the deviation is from the norm. For example, the interest rate for someone just out of bankruptcy this month will be different than the rate quoted for the potential borrower who has had sporadic late pays in the last 12 months on credit cards and an auto loan.

> **Before You Sign** _____
>
> If you fall into the subprime category (and 1 out of 4 buyers in 2004 did), you'll need to understand another way of thinking, the alternative to what we've discussed so far. The subprime loan is meant to be a temporary loan, a bandage to allow you some time to heal. And once the damage begins to correct itself, a good lender will refinance you into a more streamlined loan program, typically within 18 to 24 months.

A higher rate shouldn't be construed as a bad thing. Keep in mind that until a few years ago, if you had walked into the lender with a recent bankruptcy, your options would have been next to none. The lender would have told you to go home until at least two years had elapsed since the bankruptcy discharge and you had re-established credit. Even then, your choices would have been very limited.

Just because you choose to finance your home with a subprime loan doesn't mean you're locked into the loan forever. The idea behind alternative financing is to give you a financing option if you need or want to buy today. As your circumstances improve over the next 18 to 24 months, a good loan officer will encourage you to consider refinancing for better terms. Make certain that you're familiar with any consequences if the loan is paid off early and what, if any, penalties you may incur.

Predatory Lending: What It Is and How to Identify It

Subprime loans have provided money for many people who would not otherwise have been able to buy a house. That's the positive side of the subprime market. But unfortunately, some unsavory lenders take advantage of clients who have less-than-perfect credit. And unknowingly, borrowers have found themselves in loans that they cannot afford but that are too expensive to get out of.

Predatory lending is the practice of making high-cost home loans to borrowers without considering the borrower's ability to repay the loan. It's important to keep in mind that although subprime lenders charge higher fees for their services than do conforming lenders, not all subprime lending is considered predatory.

Predatory lending is classified by the U.S. Department of Housing and Urban Development as abusive practices in the mortgage-lending market, such as charging excessive interest rates and fees, or making prepayment penalties so high that a borrower cannot afford to refinance or sell his or her home.

Each state has its own definition of what is considered predatory, and they all have their ways of dealing with the growing problem. But for the consumer, if the loan sounds too expensive, it probably is—so keep looking!

And don't assume for one minute that if you have good credit and income you're safe from the possibility of being taken advantage of. Even the most creditworthy and knowledgeable clients could find themselves in a fraudulent loan situation. The message here is to ask the right questions and get everything in writing far enough in advance of your closing date to make educated decisions.

Several types of predatory activity exist. Here are a few:

◆ Requiring buyers to pay more for a home than it's worth, so the buyers cannot sell it for what they owe.

◆ Quoting a different (lower) rate and terms for a loan at application, and then actually charging a higher rate or terms at closing.

◆ Selling buyers on a payment without considering the fees and expenses that go along with the loan. Often the higher fees mean that it will take buyers longer to recover the cost of the refinance even if the payment is lowered.

◆ Increasing buyers' mortgage balance for debt consolidation. This can put a borrower in a position of owing more than they can afford on their home.

♦ Asking buyers to send advance fees to "guarantee" a rate or program before they receive any loan information because the rate or program is about to change.

The lower the interest rates fall, the more frequent the incidence of predatory activity. Some lenders even go so far as to steal a homeowner's equity through high fees during refinancing.

The Effects of Predatory Lending

Rising home values nationwide have escalated the incidence of predatory lending. Because homes are worth more, there is more opportunity for a lender to suggest using the home as a vehicle for debt consolidation The risk is that should you need to sell the home in the future, you are limiting the amount available for your next purchase. Remember, the equity in your home is a savings account. When you use your equity to pay off other debt or cover closing costs to refinance, you're in effect spending your savings.

Homeowners aren't the only ones who suffer from the effects of predatory lending. Entire communities suffer when borrowers cannot afford to maintain their house payments or keep up on the home maintenance because their house payment is so high. When property is foreclosed upon, adjacent properties and even entire neighborhoods may experience reduced property values. As property values decrease, equity throughout the community diminishes.

Legitimate lenders also suffer from predatory lending practices. Many of the loans that are initiated under predatory circumstances are then sold to larger, respectable companies. As defaults and foreclosures rise, so does the cost of doing business within the entire organization. Eventually, the extra expenses are filtered back to future consumers in the form of higher rates. The only winner is the original lender, who walks away with a pocket full of cash.

How to Avoid Predatory Lending

Here are tips on how to be a better consumer and avoid the predatory lender:

◆ Take a credit-counseling class to educate yourself on money matters, as they relate to both owning a home and your personal finances.

◆ Shop around when looking for a lender and a real estate agent. Talk to several people before choosing one to work with, and be wary of anyone who refers you to only one person to talk to.

◆ Request information from your real estate agent on the prices of homes in the area you are interested in. Check out both the initial asking price and the sale price to ensure that you're paying a fair market value.

◆ Hire a licensed home inspector to examine the home on your behalf. And negotiate up front who is responsible for the repairs, if any are needed.

Before You Sign

A home inspection is highly recommended on any home you purchase. The inspector will report concerns within the home as well as make maintenance suggestions. But to be a home inspector does not require a license in many states. So when shopping for a reputable, qualified inspector, consult www.nachi.org for a list of questions to ask before hiring.

◆ Keep in mind that subprime loans are meant to be temporary and refinanced to a conforming loan product within 18 to 24 months. Watch out for high prepayment penalties if the loan is rewritten in the first few years.

◆ Read all paperwork carefully, and never sign a blank document. If you don't understand what you are reading, ask for help. The Department of Housing and Urban Development (HUD) has a list of counselors available at low/no cost who can offer advice and assistance. Visit their website at www.hud.org for the name of a counselor near you.

◆ Before refinancing, compare your current monthly payment and final loan balance to the proposed new payment and balance.

A cheaper monthly payment doesn't mean it's a better deal, particularly if there are a lot of fees associated with the refinance that make the loan balance climb.

- Go with your gut instincts: if the loan fees sound high, they probably are! Keep looking.

- Be realistic about what you can and cannot afford. Just because a lender tells you that you can afford something doesn't mean your lifestyle will support it.

- If you are in a vulnerable financial state, be extra careful in the decisions you make. Take time to make decisions, and don't be pressured to act too quickly.

- If the lender tells you he or she is the only one who can help you, keep looking!

- If you don't know anything about the lender, check with the Better Business Bureau and the state regulatory agency that governs lenders in your area for a reference.

- Keep in mind that minorities and the elderly are often targets of predatory lending practices.

Because of the increasing incidence of predatory lending, the lending industry as a whole has come under significant scrutiny. People are beginning to demand that Congress enact federal anti–predatory lending legislation. Lawmakers agree that it should be forbidden to take advantage of a captive and often desperate audience, or to target a group of borrowers who might feel unable to overcome their circumstances by any other means than to pay exorbitant fees.

Fortunately, several federal mandates are in place that state what each lender is required to provide in the loan program. Regulatory agencies that oversee lending operations are diligent in their audits, carefully reviewing lenders' disclosure practices to make sure that they are accurate and reflect the true costs of doing business. These forms offer the client the opportunity to compare rates, as you will see in Chapter 7.

The Least You Need to Know

♦ Predatory loans are often subprime, but not all subprime loans are predatory.

♦ Loan credit categories range from A to C, with A being the best and B/C being less than perfect. Expect the cost of your loan to go up as your credit rating goes down.

♦ Predatory lenders take advantage of a homeowner or buyer by charging higher fees and showing no regard for the client's ability to repay the obligation.

Chapter 7

Understanding the Costs of Doing Business

In This Chapter

- ◆ Getting an estimate of the costs
- ◆ Itemizing the financed amount
- ◆ Learning the truth about the APR

It has been said that the only thing a lender doesn't ask for in the loan application is your blood type. If you were lending your money to a perfect stranger, wouldn't you want to know that it was likely the loan could and would be repaid? The series of application questions and the list of required documents are simply the easiest way for a lender to get to know a prospective borrower and determine whether he is a good candidate for a loan.

But after the interview is completed and you've handed over your paperwork, the lender will provide you with several documents that explain and define the terms and conditions of the loan you've just applied for. Now it's your turn to ask the questions! This chapter will help you educate yourself on what to expect from the lender and how to read those documents and disclosures.

You will find that lenders vary in their approaches, their costs, and their products. Fortunately, government disclosure laws require all lenders to provide the same information in similar format, making it easier to make comparisons. This is especially helpful when trying to determine the cost to do business while choosing a lender.

Good Faith Estimate

In Chapter 1, we discussed the question "How much home can you afford?" When you meet with a lender and fill out a Uniform Residential Loan Application (remember that from Chapter 4?), the lender is required to provide an estimate of fees associated with obtaining a home loan, along with a reasonable estimate of the payment.

The estimate includes a breakdown of the mortgage payment showing property taxes, homeowner's insurance, and mortgage insurance, if applicable. Mortgage insurance may be required on certain loan types and is fully explained in Chapter 8. The sales price, down payment, and loan amount are shown, along with the loan-product term and interest rate. Fees are listed in categories, by lender and closing/escrow company.

It's Your Money

Escrow can have two meanings in the mortgage industry, but both refer to holding money. First, in an escrow account, the borrower impounds (with the lender) the monies necessary to pay for property taxes and any insurance required for the loan. The escrow closing refers to a third party that holds all earnest/security deposits, pending satisfaction of all closing contingencies. This party is also responsible for acting on behalf of the lender, facilitating deed transfers.

The form, known as a *Good Faith Estimate*, means that in "good faith" the lender will provide you an accurate estimate of fees you'll need at closing, or settlement. The figures are based upon the information as it is known today: sales price (or proposed sales price, in the case of a preapproval), loan amount, and customary fees for your locale. The lender will estimate the cost of all closing or settlement expenses—their own and those from other sources. A sample good faith estimate is included in this chapter.

Most likely, no two lender good faith estimates will look alike, and no two companies will list their fees in the same order or call them by the same name. But you can make an overall comparison thanks to line-item entry similarities mandated by the federal government.

Items in section 800 of the good faith estimate cover the lender charges. Item 801 is the lender's fee to do the loan.

def•i•ni•tion

Mortgage brokers are required to disclose to the borrower their **yield spread** in the 800 category. The yield is the income a broker will receive for having sent the buyer to the company providing the mortgage. When comparing lenders, consider the yield spread when making your decision. Even if you're not directly paying for the cost, your interest rate reflects the spread.

Item 802 lists any discount points, which are the costs associated with obtaining the interest rate (see Chapter 10).

Item 803 is the appraisal fee, which is often collected at the beginning of the transaction as an application fee.

Item 804 is the credit report fee, which is often collected at the beginning of the transaction as an application fee.

Item 805 is the lender's inspection fee. If any type of work requires completion prior to closing, the lender may send an inspector to verify completion.

Item 808 is the mortgage broker fee, a fee charged by brokers, which represents their *yield spread*, or gross income.

Item 809 is the tax-related service fee. Because most mortgage lenders require taxes to be paid as part of the payment, separate companies now work on contract with lenders to search tax bills at county tax assessors' offices to ensure that taxes are properly credited when paid. This is the fee for that service.

GOOD FAITH ESTIMATE

Applicants:	John Doe / Jane Doe	Application No:	cig1
Property Addr:	123 Pleasantview, Anywhere, US 55555	Date Prepared:	11/06/2005
Prepared By:		Loan Program:	30 YR FIXED

The information provided below reflects estimates of the charges which you are likely to incur at the settlement of your loan. The fees listed are estimates-actual charges may be more or less. Your transaction may not involve a fee for every item listed. The numbers listed beside the estimates generally correspond to the numbered lines contained in the HUD-1 settlement statement which you will be receiving at settlement. The HUD-1 settlement statement will show you the actual cost for items paid at settlement.

Total Loan Amount $ **166,250**   Interest Rate: **6.000** %   Term: **360 / 360** mths

800	ITEMS PAYABLE IN CONNECTION WITH LOAN:			
801	Loan Origination Fee		$	
802	Loan Discount			
803	Appraisal Fee	(PAID)	350.00	
804	Credit Report	(PAID)	35.00	
805	Lender's Inspection Fee			
808	Mortgage Broker Fee			
809	Tax Related Service Fee		75.00	PFC
810	Processing Fee		150.00	PFC
811	Underwriting Fee		100.00	PFC
812	Wire Transfer Fee			
	Flood Life of Loan Certificate		18.00	PFC
	Courier Fee		25.00	PFC

1100	TITLE CHARGES:			
1101	Closing or Escrow Fee:		$	225.00
1105	Document Preparation Fee			
1106	Notary Fees			
1107	Attorney Fees			
1108	Title Insurance:			582.00
	Title Endorsements-EPA & Survey			200.00
	Title Binder			50.00

1200	GOVERNMENT RECORDING & TRANSFER CHARGES:			
1201	Recording Fees:		$	75.00
1202	City/County Tax/Stamps:			
1203	State Tax/Stamps:			
	Assignment		20.00	PFC

1300	ADDITIONAL SETTLEMENT CHARGES:			
1302	Pest Inspection		$	
	Property Survey			150.00

		Estimated Closing Costs	2,055.00

900	ITEMS REQUIRED BY LENDER TO BE PAID IN ADVANCE:				
901	Interest for	15 days @ $	27.3288	per day	$ 409.93	PFC
902	Mortgage Insurance Premium				PFC
903	Hazard Insurance Premium			600.00	
904					
905	VA Funding Fee				

1000	RESERVES DEPOSITED WITH LENDER:				
1001	Hazard Insurance Premiums	2 months @ $	50.00	per month	$ 100.00	
1002	Mortgage Ins. Premium Reserves	0 months @ $	96.97	per month		PFC
1003	School Tax	months @ $		per month		
1004	Taxes and Assessment Reserves	2 months @ $	300.00	per month	600.00	
1005	Flood Insurance Reserves	months @ $		per month		
		months @ $		per month		
		months @ $		per month		

	Estimated Prepaid Items/Reserves	1,709.93
TOTAL ESTIMATED SETTLEMENT CHARGES		3,764.93

TOTAL ESTIMATED FUNDS NEEDED TO CLOSE:			TOTAL ESTIMATED MONTHLY PAYMENT:	
Purchase Price/Payoff (+)	175,000.00	New First Mortgage(-)	Principal & Interest	996.75
Loan Amount (-)	166,250.00	Sub Financing(-)	Other Financing (P & I)	
Est. Closing Costs (+)	2,055.00	New 2nd Mtg Closing Costs(+)	Hazard Insurance	50.00
Est. Prepaid Items/Reserves (+)	1,709.93		Real Estate Taxes	300.00
Amount Paid by Seller (-)			Mortgage Insurance	96.97
			Homeowner Assn. Dues	
			Other	
Total Est. Funds needed to close		12,514.93	Total Monthly Payment	1,443.72

These estimates are provided pursuant to the Real Estate Settlement Procedures Act of 1974, as amended (RESPA). Additional information can be found in the HUD Special Information Booklet, which is to be provided to you by your mortgage broker or lender, if your application is to purchase residential real property and the lender will take a first lien on the property.   The undersigned acknowledges receipt of the booklet "Settlement Costs," and if applicable the Consumer Handbook on ARM Mortgages.

Applicant **John Doe**	Date	Applicant **Jane Doe**	Date

Calyx Form gfe2.frm 11/01

Good faith estimate.

Item 810 is the processing fee, which a lender can charge for administering loan documentation and collecting necessary information.

Item 811 is the underwriting fee, which the lender can charge for assessing the credit risk associated with a mortgage loan.

Item 812 is a wire-transfer fee, which is a cost associated with electronically transferring money from bank to bank rather than by check.

The unnumbered "Flood Life of Loan Certification" fee determines whether a property lies within a flood plain. If it does not, the flood-determination company certifies and warrants that the property does not lie within a flood plain for the life of the loan.

The unnumbered courier fee is for express mail/overnight mail.

Items in section 1100 of the good faith estimate are estimates of fees that are actually paid to the title company or escrow agent. The lender anticipates these costs so that the borrower has an accurate estimate of monies needed to be brought to closing.

Item 1101 is the closing agent's fee for administering the paperwork at closing.

Item 1105 is the document-preparation fee for preparing legal mortgage documents.

Item 1106 is the notary fee for a notary public to acknowledge signatures.

Item 1107 is the attorney fees for a closing attorney review.

Item 1108 is affirmative insurance coverage to ensure the lender's priority lien position and to guarantee to the owner a marketable title to the property.

The unnumbered "Title Endorsements—EPA & Survey" line insures the lender against the loss in marketability of the title due to hazardous environmental conditions.

The unnumbered "Title Binder" shows the proposed insured (that is, the lender and owner), the legal names under which they will take title, the amounts of coverage, the terms under which the proposed policy will be issued, and the expiration date of the binder.

Items in section 1200 of the good faith estimate are the government recording and transfer charge fees charged by municipalities for recording documents for public records.

Item 1201 is the recording fee charged by the county recorder or clerk to make a document a matter of public record.

Item 1202 is for the city and county tax stamps.

Item 1203 is a transaction fee charged by some states when a property is conveyed or encumbered with a lien.

The unnumbered assignment fee is collected at the time of closing to process and record an assignment of rights to the mortgage from one lender to another.

Items in section 1300 are any additional settlement charges.

Item 1302 is any fees charged by a pest-control firm to determine whether there is evidence of insect infestation or dry rot.

The survey is a schematic description of where the house lies in relation to property boundaries.

Items in section 900 are payments to be set aside for the prepaid expenses of taxes, insurances, and interest, as described in Chapter 4. At closing you will be required to impound enough of each to make certain that money is available to pay taxes and insurance as they come due. The lender recalculates the amount annually; lenders are permitted to hold only what is necessary for the upcoming 12 months.

Item 901 is the dollar amount of interest per day (per diem) that you are responsible for from the date of closing through the remainder of the month in which you close. It's common for a preapproval application to reflect 15 days.

Item 902 is the mortgage insurance premium, which is financed or paid at closing on FHA loans. It is the risk insurance covering the lender (but paid or financed by the borrower) because of the lower down payments. Item 903 is the first-year hazard insurance premium, paid in advance of its use. Item 905 is the VA's funding fee to administer the loan, if applicable.

Section 1000 itemizes the amount to be deposited into the escrow account. Money is not set aside in this account arbitrarily; only funds needed to pay future installments of taxes and insurance can be escrowed, and the guidelines are enforced by federal legislation.

Item 1001 is the annual hazard insurance premium ($600 from line 903) divided by 12. $50/month is set aside if there is an impound.

Item 1002 is the mortgage insurance premium reserves, which is the risk insurance escrow impound.

Items 1003, 1004, and 1005 are covered in more detail in Chapter 3.

The total estimated settlement charges are added up.

The section on the total estimated funds needed to close is described as follows:

◆ Purchase price/payoff (+) is the price paid for the house, the balance of the mortgage for refinancing.

◆ The loan amount (–) is the amount borrowed.

◆ Estimated closing costs (+) are the fees to close from both the lender and the closing agent.

◆ Estimated prepaid items/reserves (+) are the escrow impounds and prepaid interest through the end of the month in which you close.

◆ Amount paid by seller (–) is the cash the seller has agreed contractually to contribute toward the buyer's expenses to close.

◆ Total estimated funds needed to close is the money to bring to the closing (either cashier's check or wired).

The section on the total estimated monthly payment is described as follows:

◆ Principal and interest is the amortized monthly payment representing both principal and interest.

◆ "Other Financing (P&I)" is the payment for a second mortgage if applicable.

◆ Hazard insurance is the annual hazard insurance premium divided by 12.

♦ Real estate taxes are the annual property taxes divided by 12.

♦ Mortgage insurance is the annual mortgage insurance premium divided by 12.

♦ Homeowner association dues are paid to the association, not the lender, but are included in the total monthly housing expense for qualification purposes.

♦ Anything listed under "Other" may include special assessments for sewer, paving, sidewalks, recreation districts, and so on.

♦ The total monthly payment is the amount you can expect to pay each month.

You'll incur several standard expenses when you take out a mortgage loan; we discuss the closing costs you may expect to pay in Chapter 11, when we review the *HUD-1 Settlement Statement*. But some fees charged may represent direct profit to the lender. Unscrupulous lenders may attempt to "pad" the good faith estimate with so-called "junk fees." These fees may appear as normal fees at inflated rates, or they may be altogether bogus. And when comparing programs and fees, you'll find that the descriptions may vary, making it difficult to compare. This is why the good faith estimate and its standardized format so important.

def•i•ni•tion

The HUD-1 Settlement Statement, also known as the closing statement, is the document prepared that reconciles the settlement fees for both borrowers and sellers at closing. See Chapter 11 for a sample copy of this statement.

Truth-in-Lending Disclosure Statement

Any time you borrow money, whether it is for a home or auto loan, or even for a credit card, the lender is required by law to provide you a summary of the cost of obtaining credit. Known as a *truth-in-lending disclosure*, this standard form reiterates to the consumer that there are costs associated with borrowing money other than just interest. This disclosure also points out the terms of the loan and any peculiarities to the loan, such as a prepayment penalty or a due-on-sale clause.

TRUTH-IN-LENDING DISCLOSURE STATEMENT
(THIS IS NEITHER A CONTRACT NOR A COMMITMENT TO LEND)

Applicants:　　**John Doe**　　　　　　　　　　　　　Prepared By:
　　　　　　　　Jane Doe
Property Address:　**123 Pleasantview**
　　　　　　　　Anywhere, US 55555
Application No:　**cig1**　　　　　　　　　　　　　Date Prepared: **11/06/2005**

ANNUAL PERCENTAGE RATE	FINANCE CHARGE	AMOUNT FINANCED	TOTAL OF PAYMENTS
The cost of your credit as a yearly rate	The dollar amount the credit will cost you	The amount of credit provided to you or on your behalf	The amount you will have paid after making all payments as scheduled
* 6.908 %	$ * 228,289.99	$ * 165,452.07	$ * 393,742.06

☐ REQUIRED DEPOSIT: The annual percentage rate does not take into account your required deposit
　　PAYMENTS: Your payment schedule will be:

Number of Payments	Amount of Payments **	When Payments Are Due	Number of Payments	Amount of Payments **	When Payments Are Due	Number of Payments	Amount of Payments **	When Payments Are Due
		Monthly Beginning:			Monthly Beginning:			Monthly Beginning:
359	1,093.72	01/01/2006						
1	1,096.58	12/01/2035						

☐ DEMAND FEATURE: This obligation has a demand feature.
☐ VARIABLE RATE FEATURE: This loan contains a variable rate feature. A variable rate disclosure has been provided earlier.

CREDIT LIFE/CREDIT DISABILITY: Credit life insurance and credit disability insurance are not required to obtain credit, and will not be provided unless you sign and agree to pay the additional cost.

Type	Premium	Signature	
Credit Life		I want credit life insurance.	Signature:
Credit Disability		I want credit disability insurance.	Signature:
Credit Life and Disability		I want credit life and disability insurance.	Signature:

INSURANCE: The following insurance is required to obtain credit:
☐ Credit life insurance　☐ Credit disability　☑ Property insurance　☐ Flood insurance
You may obtain the insurance from anyone you want that is acceptable to creditor
☐ If you purchase　☐ property　☐ flood insurance from creditor you will pay $　　　　　for a one year term.
SECURITY: You are giving a security interest in:
☐ The goods or property being purchased　　　☐ Real property you already own.
FILING FEES: $　　**55.00**
LATE CHARGE: If a payment is more than **15** days late, you will be charged　**5.000** % of the payment
PREPAYMENT: If you pay off early, you
☐ may　☑ will not　have to pay a penalty.
☐ may　☑ will not　be entitled to a refund of part of the finance charge.
ASSUMPTION: Someone buying your property
☐ may, subject to conditions　☑ may not　assume the remainder of your loan on the original terms.
See your contract documents for any additional information about nonpayment, default, any required repayment in full before the scheduled date and prepayment refunds and penalties
☑ * means an estimate　　☑ all dates and numerical disclosures except the late payment disclosures are estimates.
* * NOTE: The Payments shown above include reserve deposits for Mortgage Insurance (if applicable), but exclude Property Taxes and Insurance.

THE UNDERSIGNED ACKNOWLEDGES RECEIVING A COMPLETED COPY OF THIS DISCLOSURE.

John Doe　　　　　　　　(Applicant)　　(Date)　　　　**Jane Doe**　　　　　　　　(Applicant)　　(Date)

　　　　　　　　　　　　　　(Applicant)　　(Date)　　　　　　　　　　　　　　　　(Applicant)　　(Date)

　　　　　　　　　　　　　　(Lender)　　(Date)

Calyx Form - til.hp (02/95)

Truth-in-lending disclosure statement.

The truth-in-lending disclosure is helpful because it includes the following calculations (in boxes at the top of the document):

♦ Annual percentage rate

♦ Finance charge

♦ Amount financed

♦ Total of payments

def•i•ni•tion

The **annual percentage rate** (APR) is a required federal calculation that shows the cost of the mortgage yearly, based upon fees paid to obtain the loan. The APR is usually higher than the actual interest rate, and borrowers should use it to compare lenders' fees.

The *annual percentage rate (APR)* calculation is determined by taking the interest rate and adding in the finance charges that the lender will collect.

A "good deal" is when the interest rate and the annual percentage rate are close, such as the 6.0 and 6.908 in our example document. This means that you are not paying excess loan fees. The APR will rise if closing fees are high. Note that on the good faith estimate, the fees marked with "PFC" (prepaid finance charge) indicate those fees considered in the APR calculation.

The finance charge indicates the amount of interest you will pay to obtain the loan. This figure of $228,289.99 assumes that you will make every payment as agreed and will not make early prepayments to the principal. If you do pay extra principal during the life of the loan, the finance charge amount will ultimately be not as high.

The amount financed is the loan amount of $166,250 minus the prepaid finance charges of $797.93: $165,452.07. You are actually borrowing the entire amount, but the government requires the lender to reflect the amounts independently, again to show the cost of doing the loan.

Finally, the total of payments is calculated by adding the finance charge and the amount financed. If you were to prepay toward the loan principal at any time, the total would be lower (because you didn't pay as much in finance charges). You pay interest only on those monies you use for the period of time you keep them.

Itemization of Amount Financed

The annual percentage rate calculation was created to promote awareness and protect consumers from outlandish fees. Yet to most who borrow money, it makes no sense. The following Itemization of Amount Financed document helps to show what type of fees are included in the APR calculation. The fees in the top section of this form were taken directly from the good faith estimate fees marked with the PFC (prepaid finance charge) abbreviation. If you take from our example the total prepaid finance charge of $797.93 and add it to the amount financed from the truth-in-lending disclosure statement ($165,452.07), it will total the amount borrowed ($166,250.00) from the good faith estimate.

Prepaid finance expenses have been defined as costs the borrower must pay to actually obtain the loan itself (not to be confused with "closing on the loan"). The federal government wanted to make certain that borrowers are aware of what fees they are paying to actually get a mortgage. You can use the APR to compare the cost of doing business among different mortgage companies.

It's Your Money

You might notice that "Assignment" (listed after on the Itemization of Amount Financed document) is not anywhere on the good faith estimate. This fee might be incurred when the lender is transferring the loan to another institution, such as a broker. The fee is most likely lumped into a recording fee on the good faith estimate.

ITEMIZATION OF AMOUNT FINANCED

Applicants:	John Doe		Lender:	
	Jane Doe			
Property Addr:	123 Pleasantview			
	Anywhere, US 55555			
Application No:	cig1		Date Prepared: 11/06/2005	

| Total Loan Amount $ | 166,250.00 | Prepaid Finance Charge $ | 797.93 | Amount Financed $ | 165,452.07 |

ITEMIZATION OF PREPAID FINANCE CHARGE

Tax Related Service Fee			75.00
Processing Fee			150.00
Underwriting Fee			100.00
Flood Life of Loan Certificate			18.00
Courier Fee			25.00
Interest for	15 days @ $	27.3288 per day	409.93
Mortgage Insurance Premium			
Mortgage Ins. Premium Reserves	0 months @ $	96.97 per month	
Assignment			20.00
Total Prepaid Finance Charge			797.93

AMOUNT PAID ON YOUR ACCOUNT / PAID TO OTHERS ON YOUR BEHALF

Loan Origination Fee			
Loan Discount			
Appraisal Fee			350.00 (PAID)
Credit Report			35.00 (PAID)
Lender's Inspection Fee			
Mortgage Broker Fee			
Wire Transfer Fee			
Hazard Insurance Premium			600.00
VA Funding Fee			
Hazard Insurance Preminums	2 months @ $	50.00 per month	100.00
School Tax			
Taxes and Assessment Reserves	2 months @ $	300.00 per month	600.00
Flood Insurance Reserves			
Closing or Escrow Fee:			225.00
Document Preparation Fee			
Notary Fees			
Attorney Fees			
Title Insurance:			582.00
Title Endorsements-EPA & Survey			200.00
Title Binder			50.00
Recording Fees:			75.00
City/County Tax/Stamps:			
State Tax/Stamps			
Pest Inspection			
Property Survey			150.00
Total Estimated Settlement Charge			3,764.93

Applicant John Doe	Date	Applicant Jane Doe	Date

Calyx Form gfe.frm 12/96

Itemization of Amount Financed.

The Least You Need to Know

- ◆ The good faith estimate and truth-in-lending disclosure are both provided to inform the borrower of the costs to obtain credit.

- ◆ Fees will vary from lender to lender, but you can make comparisons based upon the categories established on the good faith estimate.

- ◆ The closing/settlement statement in Chapter 11 correlates with the good faith estimate as a cross-reference.

- ◆ The annual percentage rate (APR) is not the rate of interest your payment is calculated at, but rather the annualized rate if all pre-paid finance charge expenses are included in the rate.

Chapter 8

Choosing the Best Type of Loan

In This Chapter

◆ Understanding amortization

◆ Prepaying your loan

◆ Considering interest-only loans

◆ Making sense of mortgage insurance

When it comes to borrowing money to purchase your home, fear not. There's a solution for everyone—you just need to make sure you're talking to the right lender. Today an unprecedented variety of loan products and programs is available, each priced relative to the amount of risk the lender is absorbing for the transaction. No longer is homeownership only for those with picture-perfect credit and "lifers" in their occupations.

The mortgage-lending industry continues to develop innovative solutions to meet the ever-changing needs of buyers. One of the latest innovations is the interest-only loan, in which you pay only the interest on the loan for a set period of time and begin paying on the principal several months or years into the loan. We explore this loan type later in the chapter, but first let's look more closely at how a traditional loan-repayment plan is structured.

How Mortgage Loans Are Repaid: Amortization

As you explore home financing, it's important to understand the mechanics of how mortgage loans are repaid. When you make a monthly payment, unequal amounts of that payment are applied to principal and interest. A complex repayment process known as *amortization* is done on home loans. On a regular mortgage loan, interest is front-loaded. That is, when you're paying back the loan, the first several years, you're actually repaying a lot of the interest on the money and a little bit of the principal amount you borrowed. The lender gets the money lent to you returned faster than you build the equity, or savings, in the home.

def•i•ni•tion

Amortization is the repayment of a liability with a portion of the payment being applied toward the principal balance as well as toward the interest owed.

To illustrate, I've included a payment schedule for the first 36 months of a loan. The interest rate is 6 percent, and the amount borrowed is $166,250. Each monthly payment is the same, at $1,093.72. But notice how each payment is divided. For example, payment 1 has $165.50 going toward the principal. So after the first payment, you now owe the lender $166,084.50. The remaining $928.22 of your payment is the interest that the lender will receive for lending you the money. Now, granted, the lender had to pay something for the money lent to you, and there are a lot of people who touch your file while you have this loan, so I'm not saying it's a bad thing. It is, however, very important that you realize where your payment is applied each month. Notice that as you continue to pay, each month the amount applied toward principal and interest changes: the amount applied to principal increases, and the amount applied to interest decreases.

36-Month Amortization Schedule

No.	Pmt. Date	Interest Rate	Payment	Principal	Interest/MI	Remaining Balance
			-----Monthly Payment-----			
1	01/01/2006	6.000	1,093.72	165.50	928.22	166,084.50
2	02/01/2006	6.000	1,093.72	166.33	927.39	165,918.17
3	03/01/2006	6.000	1,093.72	167.16	926.56	165,751.01
4	04/01/2006	6.000	1,093.72	167.99	925.73	165,583.02
5	05/01/2006	6.000	1,093.72	168.83	924.89	165,414.19
6	06/01/2006	6.000	1,093.72	169.68	924.04	165,244.51
7	07/01/2006	6.000	1,093.72	170.53	923.19	165,073.98
8	08/01/2006	6.000	1,093.72	171.38	922.34	164,902.60
9	09/01/2006	6.000	1,093.72	172.24	921.48	164,730.36
10	10/01/2006	6.000	1,093.72	173.10	920.62	164,557.26
11	11/01/2006	6.000	1,093.72	173.93	919.76	164,383.30
12	12/01/2006	6.000	1,093.72	174.84	918.89	164,208.47
			13,124.64	2,041.53	11,083.11	

continues

36-Month Amortization Schedule   (continued)

No.	Pmt. Date	Interest Rate	------Monthly Payment------			Remaining Balance
			Payment	Principal	Interest/MI	
13	01/01/2007	6.000	1,093.72	175.71	918.01	164,032.76
14	02/01/2007	6.000	1,093.72	176.59	917.13	163,856.17
15	03/01/2007	6.000	1,093.72	177.47	916.25	163,678.70
16	04/01/2007	6.000	1,093.72	178.36	915.36	163,500.34
17	05/01/2007	6.000	1,093.72	179.25	914.47	163,321.09
18	06/01/2007	6.000	1,093.72	180.14	913.58	163,140.95
19	07/01/2007	6.000	1,093.72	181.05	912.67	162,959.90
20	08/01/2007	6.000	1,093.72	181.95	911.77	162,777.95
21	09/01/2007	6.000	1,093.72	182.86	910.86	162,595.09
22	10/01/2007	6.000	1,093.72	183.77	909.95	162,411.32
23	11/01/2007	6.000	1,093.72	184.69	909.03	162,226.63
24	12/01/2007	6.000	1,093.72	185.62	908.10	162,042.01
			13,124.64	2,167.46	10,957.18	

continues

36-Month Amortization Schedule   (continued)

No.	Pmt. Date	Interest Rate	Monthly Payment			Remaining Balance
			Payment	Principal	Interest/MI	
25	01/01/2007	6.000	1,093.72	186.54	907.18	161,854.47
26	02/01/2007	6.000	1,093.72	187.48	906.24	161,666.99
27	03/01/2007	6.000	1,093.72	188.42	905.30	161,478.57
28	04/01/2007	6.000	1,093.72	189.36	904.36	161,289.21
29	05/01/2007	6.000	1,093.72	190.30	903.42	161,098.91
30	06/01/2007	6.000	1,093.72	191.26	902.46	160,907.65
31	07/01/2007	6.000	1,093.72	192.21	901.51	160,715.44
32	08/01/2007	6.000	1,093.72	193.17	900.55	160,522.27
33	09/01/2007	6.000	1,093.72	194.14	899.58	160,328.13
34	10/01/2007	6.000	1,093.72	195.11	898.61	160,133.02
35	11/01/2007	6.000	1,093.72	196.08	897.64	159,936.94
36	12/01/2007	6.000	1,093.72	197.07	896.65	159,739.87
			13,124.64	2,301.14	10,823.50	

This amortization schedule in its entirety would reflect all 360 payments for this 30-year loan. As you continue down the partial schedule, the remaining balance, or principal, continues to decrease. At the end of the thirty-sixth payment, you now owe the lender $159,739.87. You will have paid $2,301.14 toward the principal reduction, while the lender will have received $10,823.50 in interest payments. In the first three years, 21 percent of what you paid to the mortgage holder was applied toward the amount you actually borrowed.

This is how all mortgage amortization is structured. The variables are the interest rate, the amount borrowed, and the number of years you sign up to repay the loan.

It's Your Money

As you look at the amortization table, you'll notice the interest expense going down over the years. This means that more of your payment is going to actually pay off the mortgage principal and build equity in your home. It also means that your interest expense and interest expense tax deduction go down over the years.

Duration of the Loan: Loan Term

Now let's look at how the term impacts the loan. The term, or duration of the loan, is the amount of time you will be in debt to the lender. The term you select impacts your payment and total interest paid on the loan. If you want to keep your money invested outside of your home, you pick a longer term. If you want to own your home quickly and have your money invested in your home, you pick a shorter term.

As you learned from Chapter 1, most borrowers back into the payment they want, based upon their monthly income and comfort level. Today 30-year loans are common. That's not to say that you cannot find a 15-year loan or extend a loan for up to 40 years. But consider what might happen if, rather than borrowing for 30 years, you choose a shorter loan repayment.

Remember, as you repay a loan, you're increasing your house's "savings account." So it stands to reason that the faster you can pay back a loan, the more money you have saved in your home. The figures in the following table are all assuming the same 6 percent interest rate and loan amount of $166,250. Note, however, that in real life, the shorter the term is, the lower the rate you should receive. The interest rate on a 20-year mortgage should be lower than for a 30-year mortgage taken out on the same day. This example is only to illustrate a point and keep all variables the same.

These figures are all assuming a 6% interest rate, on a loan amount of $166,250 and the Principal and Interest Paid amounts are after 36 months of scheduled payments					
Loan Term	Monthly P&I Payment	Total of 36 Payments	Principal Amount Paid	Interest Amount Paid	Remaining Loan Balance
15 year	$1,402.91	$50,504.76	$22,486.96	$28,017.80	$143,763.04
20 year	$1,191.07	$42,878.52	$14,153.78	$28,724.74	$152,096.22
25 year	$1,071.15	$38,561.40	$9,436.77	$29,124.63	$156,813.23
30 year	$996.75	$35,883.00	$6,510.23	$29,372.77	$159,739.77
40 year	$914.73	$32,930.28	$3,283.82	$29,646.46	$162,966.18

Whether you decide on 30 or 15 years depends upon your savings preferences. You will want to consider the overall impact the mortgage plays in your long-term financial goals. A home is only one of several assets you will and should collect in your lifetime, and it is usually one of the least liquid; that means you cannot always put your hands on the money you have invested into it.

Diversity is key in any savings plan. As you plan for the future, it's important to not have all of your eggs in one basket. During times that you can get a good return, you might want to invest some of your money outside of your home in a mutual fund or stocks. And you'll find that as one investment value is going down, another is increasing. If stocks are up, property value may be down. If you diversify your investments, the ebb and flow of any given investment should not impact dramatically your financial well-being.

As you plan for retirement, it's very important to take advantage of all types of investments and their returns. To help you decide what is best for you when it comes to your home mortgage, answer the following questions:

◆ How much interest will you pay to borrow the money? Can you earn more than you're paying to borrow the money?

- How much has the home appreciated (increased in property value) over the last 12 to 24 months? If historically the market is increasing by 3 to 5 percent annually, can you do a whole lot better if you invest elsewhere?

- Do you have a balanced portfolio? In other words, do you have fixed assets, such as certificates of deposit, along with more aggressive funds, such as mutual funds?

- Do you have other reserves, or is the equity in your home your primary savings account?

- Can you afford to pay a higher loan payment monthly if you want fewer years on the loan?

When you've answered these questions, if you still aren't sure what term is right for your situation, sit down with a financial advisor and ask him or her to guide you to a decision.

Prepayment Options

So let's say you don't want to tie yourself into the higher monthly payment of a 15- or 20-year loan, but you like the idea of watching the balance you owe go down more than what a typical 30-year loan payment reduces it. As part of your lender interview worksheet (from Chapter 2), you'll notice the questions "Is there a penalty if I prepay?" and "Can I pay extra principal?" No matter what type of loan you're looking at, I always recommend that you discuss the option of prepayment. Prepaying means that the lender has given you permission to pay the minimum payment each month plus an additional amount of your choosing, which is applied toward the principal.

Some lenders will fine you or charge you a prepayment penalty if you try to pay extra each month or if you pay off the outstanding balance early. Remember, the lender makes money each month that you have that loan. And in some cases, they want to discourage you from paying it off any sooner than they would break even from a profit standpoint (for example, if they made the loan at a deeply discounted initial interest rate). So always ask the question "Is there any penalty for prepayment,

either monthly or if I decide to pay off the entire balance with a refinance?" and confirm the answer even before signing the final documents.
Examine the note for the prepayment clause. Also, the truth-in-lending
disclosure statement discussed in Chapter 7 has a box the lender needs to
mark if the penalty exists.

Calculating Payments on Your Own Using Excel

The amortization tables (see Appendix B) at the back of the book are
a handy way to quickly determine a payment for a mortgage loan you
are considering. Another fun way to get exact information without
using a table or calling up your mortgage broker is to use the Excel
spreadsheet functions.

Let's do one together. Let's say you are considering a 30-year, 6 percent
loan of $200,000, and you want to know how much your payment would
change if you wait for rates to drop to 5 percent.

Using Microsoft Excel, your entries would be:

1. Click the fx **Paste Function** button on the Standard toolbar.

2. Choose the Function category **Financial.**

3. Choose the Function name **payment.**

4. Click **OK.**

5. Enter the rate **.06/12** (.06 is the interest rate and 12 is to give you
   a monthly payment).

6. Enter the NPER **30*12** (360 for the number of months in 30
   years of monthly payments; this would be 180 for a 15-year loan).

7. Enter the PV **200000** (amount you want to finance).

8. Click **OK.**

The dialog box returns –$1,432.86. Notice that it is a negative number.
This is a convention used in this type of financial calculation. If it both-
ers you, you can enter the amount of the loan as a negative number,
and the payment will read as a positive number.

Typing over the numbers in the Rate box to make it .05/12 changes the result to $1,319.91. This allows you to compare your two interest rates. If you move down one cell, you can save both calculations for later review.

As you play with closing costs, interest rates, and terms of loans, this simple tool in Excel can give you instant, accurate information to help you make the best decisions. If you don't have a computer with Excel already loaded, chances are your library or a friend does. There are also a lot of payment calculators on personal finance websites, but none is as convenient or fast as this one. Also, by moving from cell to cell in your spreadsheet, you can save your calculations and make notes next to each as you compare various loan packages.

If you don't have access to a computer, fear not. In the back of the book are the amortization factors and a neat explanation of how to calculate a payment.

Interest-Only Loans

Lenders regularly devise new loan programs to meet new needs. As stock prices plummeted in recent years, investors took big losses on their portfolios and money started to shift. Real estate began to look like a better investment, and property started to increase in value. And as property values climbed, so did the equity in the home. The client owned more of the home, and the lending community felt good about its loan positions.

Because property was appreciating at a good pace, interest-only loans became available to homebuyers. Although they're not an entirely new lending concept, to require that only interest be paid to borrow money on a house opened up a whole new market for lenders. Because the lender isn't requiring the loan to be repaid, the risk is a bit higher, and so is the interest rate. Lenders like these loans because they can charge a higher interest rate. Homebuyers like them because the payment is lower without the principal reduction on amortized loans. And the concept is widely endorsed by financial planners and money managers because if your payment is lower, ideally the consumer can be convinced to divert the monthly savings into investments.

Although the lender isn't asking the borrower to repay the loan immediately, repayment is required at some point. For example, if the loan is a 30-year loan, the lender may allow you to make interest-only payments for 10 years, but once you reach month 120, the lender will likely increase the payment to ensure that the loan is paid out in the remaining 20 years of the loan.

Before You Sign

Because interest-only home mortgage loans are relatively new, the lending community hasn't really evaluated how they perform and the risk they pose. It's likely that as the economic climate changes and real estate values taper, terms and conditions will change as needed. Remember, lending is a fluid industry. But for now, the option to either amortize and pay toward the balance or pay only interest is available.

Now that you understand the mechanics of how a mortgage loan is repaid and what an interest-only feature can do, it is time to explore the different loan programs available. Lenders may or may not offer each of the programs we review, so once you zero in on a loan solution that feels right, you may find yourself gravitating toward specific lenders that offer your chosen loan solution.

Loan Categories: FHA, VA, Conventional

Before you begin your search for loan solutions, it's important to familiarize yourself with the categories of loans available.

The basic loan categories for conforming loans are FHA (Federal Housing Administration), VA (Veteran's Administration), and conventional mortgage loans. The next segment of this chapter educates you on each type. We compare the loans for you, to help you decide which may be the most likely to suit your needs. Not every loan category has the same specifications; at the same time we're offering comparison, understand that all three require different documentation and different requirements. For example, if you are eligible for a VA home loan, you'll find details that will aid you in getting yourself prepared to finance. And based upon general guidelines, you will see why the lender may recommend FHA financing over a VA loan.

There's a lot of great information in this section about both FHA and VA mortgages. Because they are regulated by government agencies, there are more requirements and regulations than for conventional mortgages. But don't let the requirements discourage you from applying for the government loans; a lot of people couldn't buy a home without these tremendous loan solutions.

FHA Mortgage Loans

The Federal Housing Administration (FHA) helps banks lend to buyers who don't have a great deal of money. FHA allows a borrower to purchase with as little as a 3 percent cash investment. The program was started in 1934 to rebuild and update homes to stimulate the economy after World War II. The FHA itself is not a lender. Instead, it "assures" lenders that they will receive repayment, even if the borrower *defaults*, or doesn't pay on the loan. How can the FHA do this, you might ask? The FHA offers the lender an insurance, *which the borrower pays for*, known as MIP (mortgage insurance premium).

Mortgage Insurance Premiums (MIP)

FHA mortgage insurance premiums have been modified over the years. When the program began, premiums were paid on a monthly basis, calculated at .50 times the loan amount divided by 12 months. Today that calculation is still valid; however, the program realized a severe shortage in funds in the late 1980s, and an additional premium was added to increase revenues in the early 1990s. Using a $100,000 mortgage example, here is how you can expect the insurance to be calculated today:

> Mortgage amount, also known as base loan ($100,000) × MIP financed (1.5%) = $1,500. The total loan amount is calculated by adding the base loan ($100,000) to the MIP amount ($1,500) to get $101,500.

> Mortgage amount ($100,000) × MIP monthly (.50) = $500 MIP yearly. The FHA uses the base loan amount to calculate the monthly premium.

> $500 MIP yearly ÷ 12 months = $41.67 per month

The MIP insurance can be compared to the private mortgage insurance for conventional loans, and is discussed in the "Private Mortgage Insurance (PMI)" section later in this chapter. Unlike PMI, the FHA's MIP insurance is mandatory regardless of how much money a borrower puts into the property. The FHA requires the insurance be collected until the borrower has paid down the original loan balance to 78 percent and for no less than five years.

FHA loans were created as first-time-buyer loans, and although they've been used repeatedly as such, they are not exclusively for that purpose. Because the required cash investment is 3 percent of the sales price, the FHA can be a nice loan solution for someone who doesn't have a lot of money or is not interested in putting as much into the purchase. And if the money for the down payment is from a gift, perhaps from a parent or relative, the FHA may be the best solution. FHA guidelines do not require borrowers to use any of their own savings for the purchase.

Because the FHA does not require a great deal of cash to purchase a home, we've recommended the loan to clients who are selling their existing home and buying another one. These people usually have a fair amount of equity in their present residence, but also have a good bit of monthly debt. In this type of scenario, we might suggest that the borrower take part of the proceeds they'll realize from their sale, pay off debt, and keep available the 3 percent they need to purchase their next home. In most cases, the client realizes a better cash flow. And the client has traded non-tax-deductible interest (on other debts) for mortgage interest, which also puts them into a better tax position.

The FHA will also allow the borrower to finance a portion of the closing costs or add them into the loan. Overall, the FHA can allow for a smaller cash outlay.

FHA Government Regulations

The FHA highly regulates its lending practices; it has set maximum mortgage limits based upon median housing expenses within each region of the country. Therefore, when considering FHA financing, you should investigate the maximum allowable loan limits for your area. The FHA has an easy-to-use and informative website at www.hud.gov. Scroll through the "Information for Homebuyers" section for the maximum mortgage limit for your area.

The government statute that put the FHA into place set up different loan types, each described in the act. 203(b) loans are the most common. They were established for one- to four-family owner-occupied purchases. Other sections include the 703(b), which was recently added to allow for loans to be done on condominiums, and the 203(k) loans, which allow funding for home renovation as part of a purchase or refinance. Not as often seen but also available are the 203(i), which is the program designated for financing manufactured housing, and a 221(d)2 loan, which allows for a modified down-payment structure for low- to moderate-income households.

A big change as of January 2006 is how FHA will evaluate the property. Historically, the appraiser was instructed to point out deficiencies in the home, such as peeling paint, broken concrete in sidewalks, broken seals on windows, and so on. Well and septic and termite inspections were also required. A list of repair items and inspections was then presented with the report, and the value was based upon completion of the items. The thought was that because the borrower was usually getting into the home on a shoestring budget, if the work could be done prior to the loan closing, the home was in better shape and a more sound investment for all. Sellers were wary of what the appraiser might ask for, so many times they would refuse an FHA offer because of this process.

Because housing market tolerance has changed, FHA has backed off of many of their previous requirements. This is good for the negotiation process as a whole because it gives buyers and sellers the option of whether they want to do work to the house before closing. But it also means that a buyer may have a few more maintenance issues today than they did previously on the same shoestring budget. The FHA provides both fixed-rate and adjustable-rate loans. For a complete explanation of financing programs and how they work, see Chapter 9.

VA Loans

The VA (Veterans Administration) was established as part of the Veterans Bill of Rights in 1944. In return for their service to our country, eligible veterans were given the opportunity to borrow 100 percent of the sales price of a home.

A VA loan is available to enlisted service personnel with continuous service for 181 days, a veteran with an honorable discharge, and any surviving spouse of an enlisted soldier killed in the line of duty. POW/ MIA surviving spouses are also eligible once the veteran is POW/MIA for 90 days. The list of eligible veterans was expanded in the 1990s to include reservists with 6-plus years of service or those enlisted who have seen active duty for 90-plus days during wartime.

The following table addresses each wartime requirement. This table is *not* exhaustive, and a veteran's eligibility for home loan benefits may be determined only by the VA, so consider this as just a guide to determining eligibility.

Era	Dates	Time Required
WWII	9/16/40 to 7/25/47	90 days
Post-WWII	7/26/47 to 6/26/50	181 days
Korean	6/27/50 to 1/21/55	90 days
Post-Korean	2/01/55 to 8/04/64	181 days
Vietnam*	8/05/64 to 5/07/75	90 days
Post-Vietnam	5/08/75 to 9/07/80	Enlisted 181 days
	5/08/75 to 10/16/81	Officers 181 days
	9/08/80 to 08/01/90	Enlisted 2 years**
	10/17/81 to 08/01/90	Officers 2 years**
Persian Gulf	8/02/90 to present	2 years

*The Vietnam Era began on 2/28/61 for those who served in the Republic of Vietnam.
**The veteran must have served 2 years or the full period of his orders, at least 90 days during wartime and 181 during peacetime.

To exercise their entitlement for a VA home loan, the veteran (or lender on behalf of the veteran) requests a certificate of eligibility from the VA. The certificate is needed because it tells the lender how much money the VA is willing to guarantee on the transaction. You can find and print this form at www.vba.va.gov/pubx/forms/_26-1800.pdf. The form should be completed and signed by the veteran, and sent to the VA with evidence of military duty. Each branch of the armed forces issues a statement of service for enlisted personnel, or discharge papers known as a DD-214. The DD-214 lists the timeline that the veteran has been in service and provides the evidence the VA requires to process the certificate.

VA Funding Fee

The VA charges veterans participating in the program a VA funding fee. The fee can be paid up front as part of the loan settlement or added on to the loan amount and financed. The amount of this fee depends upon whether the veteran is enlisted personnel or a reservist, and whether the veteran previously used the benefit. The following table lists the fees for various categories of veterans.

VA Funding Fee Tables

Purchase and Construction Loans

Type of Veteran	Down Payment	Percent of First Time Use	Percent for Subsequent Use
	DP%	FTU%	SU%
Regular	None	2.15	3.30*
military	5 to 10	1.50	1.50
	+10	1.25	1.25
Reserve/	None	2.40	3.30*
Nat'l Guard	5 to 10	1.75	1.75
	+10	1.50	1.50

Cash-Out Refinance

Regular military		2.15	3.30*
Reserve/ Nat'l Guard		2.40	3.30*

Other Loans

Interest rate reduction refinance loan		.50	.50
Manufactured home		1.00	1.00
Loan assumptions		.50	.50

*An exception is if the veteran's prior use of entitlement was for a manufactured home loan.

A veteran can use entitlement more than once only under these circumstances:

1. The original VA loan was paid in full. This includes a home that had a loan but was sold, and the loan was paid off.

2. The original VA loan was assumed by a veteran, who then substituted his or her entitlement for the other veteran's. Assumable loans are discussed in detail in Chapter 9.

The VA benefit was created to assist veterans with home purchases and, therefore, is permitted only for owner-occupied purchases.

VA Qualifying Guidelines

Qualifying guidelines for VA loans include the typical review of income, assets, credit, and ratio calculations, but the veteran must also show a certain amount of disposable money left at the end of each month. The residual income, or money left after paying the bills, is calculated by adding the total monthly housing expenses (see Chapter 1), utilities, maintenance expenses, and all long-term debt. This number is then subtracted from the veteran's net income (after-tax take-home income). The minimum amount depends upon what region of the country, the sales price, and the number of household members.

Table of Residual Income by Region (Loans $79,999 and Below)

Family Size	Northeast	Midwest	South	West
1	$390	$382	$382	$425
2	$654	$641	$641	$713
3	$788	$772	$772	$859
4	$888	$868	$868	$967
5*	$921	$902	$902	$1,104

*Over 5 add $75 for each additional member up to 7.

Table of Residual Income by Region (Loans $80,000 and Over)

Family Size	Northeast	Midwest	South	West
1	$450	$441	$441	$491
2	$755	$738	$738	$823
3	$909	$889	$889	$990
4	$1,025	$1,003	$1,003	$1,117
5*	$1,062	$1,039	$1,039	$1,158

Over 5 add $80 for each additional member up to 7.

Region geographic areas for proceeding charts:

♦ **Northeast:** Connecticut, Maine, Massachusetts, New Hampshire, New Jersey, New York, Pennsylvania, Rhode Island, Vermont

♦ **Midwest:** Illinois, Indiana, Iowa, Kansas, Michigan, Minnesota, Missouri, Nebraska, North Dakota, Ohio, South Dakota, Wisconsin

♦ **South:** Alabama, Arkansas, Delaware, District of Columbia, Florida, Georgia, Kentucky, Louisiana, Maryland, Mississippi, North Carolina, Oklahoma, Puerto Rico, South Carolina, Tennessee, Texas, Virginia, West Virginia

♦ **West:** Alaska, Arizona, California, Colorado, Hawaii, Idaho, Montana, Nevada, New Mexico, Oregon, Utah, Washington, Wyoming

Unlike FHA (MIP) and conventional financing (PMI), the VA has no insurance premium. Instead, the VA offers a *guarantee* to the lender that it will reimburse a loss up to a certain percentage of the overall loan amount if the veteran defaults. The loan benefit is good on only a single-family or multiunit dwelling that is owner occupied. And the certificate of eligibility spells out to the lender the amount that will be covered if the veteran is not able to make the home loan payments.

The distinctive benefit to the VA is that no money is needed for the down payment. The VA is very protective of its program, and has gone so far as to state what fees the borrower can and cannot pay. When considering a VA mortgage loan, you will be asking the seller to pay a portion of your loan expenses. Depending upon your purchase contract negotiation, veterans can often find themselves with no money needed at the loan closing. They can ask the seller through negotiations to pay 100 percent of their fees.

The maximum loan amount for a VA loan depends upon the conduit the lender uses for the mortgage in the secondary market and what the loan is being used for. If GNMA is used today for a purchase, the maximum is the same limit as the conventional loans noted later in this chapter. A handy website to check for current limits is www.ginniemae.gov. Note that the maximum loan must also include the VA funding fee. Most VA loans are financed with a fixed term, usually 15 or 30 years.

> **It's Your Money**
>
> Did you know? Both FHA and VA have great websites that can provide you with answers on what they have available for home loans. The VA can be accessed at www.homeloans.va.gov/eligibility.htm, and the FHA at www.hud.gov.

Conventional Mortgages

Conventional mortgage loans are traditional financing solutions dating back to the late 1800s. Today conventional financing refers to loans without government-sponsored guarantees made by commercial lenders. For many decades, loans were done only when borrowers could provide significant down payments. As FHA and VA financing became more popular because they required less of a cash investment, they took business away from the traditional lenders. Banks and thrifts needed to become more competitive in their lending practices if they hoped to compete in the home-lending arena. With the help of the *private mortgage insurance* industry, lenders became confident that they had backing and were willing to hedge their risks on loans with lower down payments.

Private Mortgage Insurance (PMI)

Conventional loans also have come a long way. Loans that once needed a minimum 50 percent down payment today can be done with no money down. The private mortgage insurance (PMI) industry developed because more borrowers wanted conventional loans but didn't have large down payments. Mimicking the FHA's insurance, these companies created a premium plan that would afford them the revenue needed to insure the loss if the borrower could not meet his or her obligation. And as with FHA loans, if a loan is not paid back to the lender, this insurance guarantees that the lender receives a percentage of the default amount.

The private mortgage insurance premium is calculated as a percentage of the loan amount. For example, for a loan with a down payment of 5 percent, the insurance will be higher than for a loan with a 10 or 15 percent down payment. And the insurance may be different for each type of loan product, such as adjustable rate or balloon (see Chapter 9 for details on these loan programs). The premium can be either financed or paid monthly.

Historically, PMI has been required on loans with less than a 20 percent down payment. It is paid begrudgingly because there is no perceived benefit to the borrower. Although the insurance allows the borrower to buy with a lower down payment, there still is the additional monthly obligation added to the house payment. Some innovative loan solutions introduced into the marketplace the last few years give the borrower another way to go. Lenders frequently offer a first and second mortgage combination loan to avoid PMI, as well as a slightly higher rate of interest instead of PMI. Chapter 10 has a section devoted to avoiding the PMI, if you are inclined to do so.

Unlike FHA/MIP, the premium either will be 100 percent financed or will be paid monthly. And there are ways to avoid mortgage insurance completely on a conventional loan, whereas the FHA's insurance is mandatory. If you need to take a loan that requires mortgage insurance, it may be possible after a couple of years to remove the insurance. You can always rewrite the loan (refinances are covered in Chapter 13) for a new loan if the lender determines by a property appraisal that you have 20 to 25 percent equity in your home. You may also petition the lender for the mortgage insurance to be removed. Specific guidelines for removing insurance protect both the lender and the borrower.

The lender will consider your petition to remove the insurance if you meet all of the following conditions:

- ◆ You have been occupying the home at least 12 to 24 months.

- ◆ You have made payments as agreed.

- ◆ You still reside in the property.

- ◆ There is proof that the home value is high enough in relation to the loan to warrant removal of the insurance.

The lender will request an appraisal or the equivalent to substantiate value. It must be stressed here that the lender's discretion determines whether the insurance will be removed.

Other Conventional Triggers

As you compare lending solutions, a few other triggers may help determine your financing path. For example, several of the *conventional* loan programs still require that you save some of the down payment on your own rather than borrow the funds from another source or receive a gift. The FHA lets you obtain 100 percent gift, if needed, and the VA has no cash requirements. Down-payment requirements are discussed in detail in Chapter 10, and you'll learn that the amount and source of funds you have available very often determine the best loan solution for you.

The amount you need to borrow may also determine the loan solution. Conventional loan limits are based upon national median mortgage sales and are adjusted normally toward the end of the year. FHA and VA loan limits have not kept pace with the conventional loans. Currently, as of 2005, the maximum *conforming* loan limits are as follows:

def•i•ni•tion

The term **conventional** refers to loans that follow the same pattern, having some conformity. You will hear these loans also referred to as **conforming** loans. Therefore, for loans that perhaps have atypical circumstances, you might find it necessary to look at "nonconforming" alternative solutions or subprime loans.

Single family	$417,000
Two units	$533,850
Three units	$645,300
Four units	$801,950

These limits are set nationally, with exceptions being Alaska, Hawaii, Guam, and the U.S. Virgin Islands. Their limits are 1.5 times the set amount.

The next logical question is "But what about loans that are higher than these limits?" Any loans beyond these limits are referred to as jumbo loans, also known as nonconforming loans. This is another time you may hear the term *nonconforming* used, but to a certain degree it makes sense. The loan limit does not meet the "norm," that being $417,000 or lower.

Jumbo loans are available for any loan above the conforming limit, but there can be a few differences. The market is somewhat limited for these products, meaning that not as many lenders offer financing solutions for these clients. Jumbo loan rates are typically higher than those for conforming loan amounts due to the greater risk the lender takes in making this type of loan.

The loan guidelines may also change, although they are not unlike the conforming loans. The lender may require greater down payments on some loans; whereas 5 percent is standard on conventional financing, some loan programs may require 10 percent in this category. Income, asset, and credit expectations, however, should not differ.

Conventional financing also differs in another way. There are more choices of loan programs to choose from. Lenders are able to more readily develop loan solutions based upon changing economic climates and market segments. Therefore, conventional financing offers a broader range of programs than the FHA and VA. As part of your selection, you will find balloon loans, as well as a variety of adjustable-rate mortgage loan programs. As you will read in Chapter 9, each can have its own set of parameters to follow. This can make the process more confusing, but you also have more ways to tailor a loan to your specific needs.

It's Your Money

After World War II, plots of land were given to returning veterans for $1 per acre. The government thought this would not only offer veterans a place to build their homes, but it would also bolster the economy with remodeling. More than a million construction workers were out of work at the time. Many homes were built, and the economy slowly came back around, providing housing along the way.

The Least You Need to Know

◆ FHA mortgages offer an opportunity to purchase with lower cash requirements because often the closing costs can be financed.

◆ VA mortgages are appealing to eligible borrowers because they allow for 100 percent financing.

◆ When a mortgage is amortized, initially more of each payment is made toward paying back the principal balance of the loan.

◆ Lenders may provide you with the option of either amortizing the loan or paying interest only.

◆ Any prepayment of principal (also referred to as a curtailment) reduces the amount of interest paid back to the lender.

Chapter 9

Deciding on the Loan Program

In This Chapter

- ◆ Fixed- and adjustable-rate mortgages
- ◆ Balloon and graduated-payment mortgages
- ◆ Assumable loans
- ◆ Making the loan decision that's best for you

There are as many different varieties of loans as there are flavors of ice cream. And because you are making some long-range plans when buying your home, it only makes sense that you will want to explore several options.

This chapter offers general information meant to guide you in understanding the different products, but you must remember that each individual lending institution may offer its own twist.

And if you are interested in FHA financing because it requires less up-front cash or because all of the money you have on hand was given to you as a gift, not every loan listed here is eligible for FHA financing. FHA, VA, and Conventional loans each have their own loan programs and requirements.

Fixed-Rate Loans

"Fixed rate" means that the interest rate does not change, and therefore the principal and interest payment you make stays the same for the term of the mortgage note. The term refers to the number of years in which the loan will be repaid. The note is the official document or IOU stating that you owe the money you are borrowing. The amount you pay to the lender will vary only as the payments for taxes and insurance change. (Remember from Chapter 1 that taxes and insurance may be periodically adjusted as those expenses change for the respective party.)

Fixed-rate loans have a variety of different terms. Most common is the 30-year fixed, but most lenders will accept terms of 25, 20, 15, and 10 years. Recently, some companies have introduced 40-year loans. FHA, VA, and conventional loan financing all have fixed-rate loans to choose from.

People who choose the fixed-rate loan option like the predictability of the payment and never need to worry about a rising interest-rate market. But as interest rates come down, they must consider refinancing to take advantage of a lower rate or a lower payment.

As you prepay a fixed-rate mortgage, your payment never changes, as we said, but the term, or number of payments you make on the loan, decreases. You can always check your progress by charting your prepayment against an amortization schedule.

Balloon Loans

The balloon loan is structured like a fixed-rate mortgage, usually amortized for 15 or 30 years. The payments are applied to an outstanding balance each month. But balloon loans usually are set with 5-, 7-, or 10-year payoffs. At the end of the specified term, the note calls for the loan to be due and payable.

For example, on a seven-year balloon, at the end of the eighty-fourth month, the lender expects the remaining loan be paid off in its entirety.

Why would a borrower put him- or herself into such a program? These loans are appealing to homebuyers because they are usually offered by the lender at an interest rate that is 0.375 to 0.50 percent lower than the rate of a 30-year loan. In a climate of rising interest rates, such loans are more affordable and entail little risk. This type of loan is ideal for homebuyers who know that they intend to stay in the house only a short time and don't need a 30-year loan. The average homeowner owns his or her home for only five to seven years. It's no coincidence that this mortgage product has become very popular: it was designed to offer payment security for a period of time most folks are likely to stay in one property.

And if you decide you aren't ready to sell the home and move after all? Provisions in the note state that as long as you are willing to pay a small fee to the lender, you've made your payments as agreed, and you still live in the home, the lender will consider extending the loan through the remaining term for a slight rate increase. Another option is to refinance the loan. Refinancing is discussed in Chapter 11.

Adjustable-Rate Mortgage (ARM)

In an adjustable-rate mortgage (ARM), also known as a variable-rate loan, the interest rate moves—and if the rate moves, so does the monthly payment. ARM loans became popular in the late 1980s as fixed interest rates hit a whopping 18 percent. As you can imagine, the housing market was almost paralyzed. People wanted to buy homes, but very few could afford to. So the attractive lower initial rates on adjustable-rate mortgages offered by lenders became very popular, and actually helped bolster the economy.

Because of their shorter terms, a lender can afford to offer ARMs at lower rates, also known as "teaser" rates. These below-the-market interest rates usually last for a predetermined time, some as short as three months. They are meant to attract the buyers who might otherwise put off their purchase until they perceive themselves to be better qualified to buy.

But don't forget that the rate is meant to be low for only a short time. It will go up. And the higher rate keeps a lot of buyers away from this type of loan. In order to decide whether ARMs are for you, it's important to learn what makes the ARM rates move around.

The Adjustments

Several different terms are available when exploring ARM loans. The adjustment schedule refers to how often you can expect the interest rate to change. Adjustable-rate loans come in all configurations, so I suggest that you ask lots of questions to educate yourself. The ARM terms will definitely vary from lender to lender, so don't expect there to be a steadfast rule. But it's not uncommon to see ARMs offered in 1-, 3-, 5-, 7-, and 10-year terms. Each "term" refers to a period of time that the loan interest will be set or fixed at a particular rate. For example, a three- and five-year ARM will have a rate fixed for three and five years, respectively.

What happens at the end of the initial fixed period? That depends upon the loan you are referring to. For example, a 3/3 ARM means that the rate is fixed for three years, and at the end of three years, the rate will be reset for another three years. A 3/1 ARM means that the rate is fixed for three years, but at the end of the three years, the rate will adjust each year. An adjustable-rate loan with a fixed period that then rolls into a one-year adjustable is also known as a hybrid ARM. The good news about ARM adjustments is that you know about them in advance, so you can prepare yourself for the movement. Certain parameters are also preset, known as adjustment *caps* and life-of-loan caps that restrict the amount that an interest rate can rise or fall. For example,

def•i•ni•tion

A **cap** on interest is the maximum rate increase allowable per the loan, as a protection to the borrower. A cap on payment is the maximum payment increase allowable per the loan, again, as a protection to the borrower.

the FHA has available a one-year ARM loan product. This means that each year the interest rate will change. The FHA has set a maximum 1 percent annual payment cap and a 5 percent lifetime cap for this loan. This means that each year your payment may move by as much as 1 percent in interest rate over what it currently is, but no more than 5 percent total.

So as a consumer, let's say your starting rate is 5 percent; next year you know your rate will be no higher than 6 percent, and the following year no higher than 7 percent. And over the entire life of the loan, your rate will be no higher than 10 percent, which is 5 percent over the starting rate. So you rarely can be caught off guard when it comes to how the rate will change. But these caps are specific to each loan. You must ask about them each time you explore a new lender's products. And although the FHA's one-year ARM is 1/5 caps, most conventional loan products are 2 percent maximum annual and 5 to 6 percent maximum over the life of the loan.

This is a great time to point out that you have some control over how the payment will move. We talked about how a prepayment on the fixed-rate loan will not affect the amount of the payment, but you will end up paying fewer months, accelerating your amortization. On an ARM loan, as you prepay, your loan balance is reduced in the same way it is on the fixed rate. But each time your interest rate is adjusted, the new payment is calculated on the outstanding principal balance at that time for the remaining term. You still have the same amortization, or number of years, to pay the loan, but your new payment will be related to how much you owe at the time.

For example, suppose that Jody is borrowing $120,000 for a condominium, knowing that she wants to move on to a home within 5 to 10 years. She has a choice of a 6.0 percent fixed rate, with a payment of $720 per month, or a 4.5 percent ARM rate with a payment of $609 per month. If she chooses the ARM loan but makes a payment equal to the fixed contract, then she will have $111 per month extra applied toward principal, or $1,332 more in equity in her condo at the end of the first year. This is money that will always be hers to add to her net worth. Even if her ARM rate increases by 1 percent the next year to 5.5 percent, her new loan payment will be calculated based upon the new loan amount of $117,150. Because she has prepaid her mortgage, Jody will never pay interest on the $1,332. Her new payment is now $665, but it is still less than the amount she would have paid on the 30-year loan, and she has created a higher net worth for herself by saving on interest expense.

So if you know you'd like to keep your payment within a range and you are financed on an ARM, try to prepay the loan balance. As the principal comes down, even if the interest rate rises, you won't feel the full effect of the increase. You can use the loan table in Appendix B to play around with different scenarios to find the one that may work for you. We review the payment calculations in the next chapter.

In order to determine how much to prepay and how much you can expect a payment to change, you must first understand what makes an ARM interest rate fluctuate.

The Index

Adjustable-rate loans typically adjust based upon the movement of some money source. This money-related item is also referred to as the *index*. As the value of this index goes up and down, so does the ARM loan rate. The following is a list of the most widely seen indexes used to set payments:

def•i•ni•tion

The **index** is the money source that drives the movement of an adjustable loan product, such as the one-three-five-year Treasury securities.

♦ **Treasury bills,** also known as **T-bills,** are used as a common indicator, also called an index, for the movement of adjustable-rate loans in the Midwest and northern regions of the country.

♦ The **11th District Cost of Funds Index** was developed to measure the rates paid to depositors on the West Coast. This index has been popular for loans in the western United States.

♦ The London Interbank Offered Rate, also known as **LIBOR,** has become a popular indicator because it is a lagging index. In other words, it is not immediately impacted by market changes.

♦ The **prime lending rate** is the rate that banks charge their best clients. The prime rate usually changes as the Federal Reserve amends its monetary policy. This is the index that directly influences what you're paid in interest from the bank and what you pay in interest on credit card debt.

The index may change hourly, daily, or weekly. But the interest rate will change only as often as its preset adjustments will allow for. If you have a volatile index, one that moves freely, then you will see your payment move more frequently.

The Margin

In all good equations, there is a variable quotient and a fixed factor. The fixed piece here is known as the *margin*. It has also been said that this is the lender's cut or profit on the loan. When shopping for an ARM loan, be sure to ask the margin because it has already been decided and will stay fixed throughout the duration of the loan. The margin can be whatever the lender feels is appropriate, but it is usually 2 to 3 percent over the amount of the current index.

def•i•ni•tion

The **margin** is the amount a lender adds to the index on an adjustable-rate mortgage to establish the interest rate; it is sometimes noted as the profit margin to the lender.

To illustrate, say that the index or money source is the U.S. Treasury Securities Index, and today it's at 3.05. A typical margin is 2.75 percent. Today's fixed-interest rate is probably 6 percent +/−. But the lender may be offering a bargain rate of 5.00 percent on a five-year ARM. And let's say that at the thirty-fifth month, the index has moved to 4.25. To determine what the new rate is, you add the current index to the always constant margin and round up to the nearest ⅛. The new rate after the third year would be 7 percent (2.75 + 4.25).

Caps

When you adjust, there are already maximum adjustments allowed because of the rate and life of loan caps. So what happens if the index-plus-margin total sum indicates that your payment should increase by 3 percent? That's the beauty of the caps—no matter what the index and margin add up to, the rate cannot exceed the caps. On the other hand, if the index and margin do not total the full adjustment amount, it's possible to move only 1 or 1.375 percent. The caps are not in place to set the rate—only to keep the rate moving within a predetermined acceptable range.

Negative Amortization and Deferred-Interest Loans

When shopping for an ARM loan, ask if the rate and the payment change at the same time. If the rate and payment move at the same time, that means you are making a payment that will allow the loan to be paid off within its term.

If, however, the rate and payment don't change at the same time, it's possible for the interest rate to go up but for the payment to stay the same. If that happens, the payment being made is probably not enough to cover the required principal and interest.

Unless you decide to pay extra each month to make up the difference, the lender will need to add on to the outstanding balance. This is called *negative amortization*, or deferred interest. In other words, you're not paying off the principal balance; instead, you're adding to the loan.

def•i•ni•tion

Negative amortization occurs when the interest rate and payment do not change at the same time. This makes the payment lower than what should adequately cover the principal and interest portions of the scheduled payment, causing more interest to accrue.

When property experiences rapid gains in value, increasing principal may not be a concern because your equity is increasing through appreciation. If, however, property values are falling or flat, you could end up owing more than the home is worth. To know whether you have a loan that could end up with deferred interest, you need to know what to look for.

Graduated-Payment Mortgage (GPM)

The graduated-payment mortgage (GPM) is a classic example of a loan with deferred interest. Like adjustable-rate mortgage loans, the graduated-payment mortgage was introduced when interest rates were as high as 18 percent in the 1980s. The GPM was designed to keep payments down so folks could afford to buy homes.

GPM loans are making a comeback in a big way today, but not because interest rates are through the roof. Housing values have risen so dramatically in many parts of the country that homeowners are realizing unprecedented appreciation.

Many borrowers began asking themselves if it made sense to pay off a loan in the traditional way and structure the payment to include principal and interest if they could earn so much equity because of this inflation in housing values. Lenders recognizing an opportunity went into the closet and dusted off the old GPM, and adapted it for today's circumstances.

The loan is set up very much like an ARM loan, in that its movement is based upon an index and a margin. But the loan itself is structured so that you start off making payments based on an artificially low teaser rate. The payment is so low that negative amortization will occur. The lender then *gradually* increases the payment based upon a predetermined schedule.

For example, let's say the index is 3.25 and the margin is 2.75. The actual rate would be 6.0. On a loan amount of $120,000, the payment would be $720.00 a month. The lender who sells the GPM may start the loan at a teaser rate of 2 percent to attract more business. The payment at 2 percent is $324. So right out of the gate, the payment you are allowed to pay is $396 short of what it would take to amortize the loan over a 30-year period. The index plus margin will continue to change monthly throughout the life of the loan. The payment will stay fixed for one year, and after the first year, the minimum payment required will rise by a predetermined amount—say, 7.5 percent—and gradually go up to $348.30 (7.5 × 324).

So the balance of the loan will increase, but if property is appreciating, then so is the value of your home.

Several lenders offer loan solutions that allow the borrower to decide how much to pay toward the loan on a monthly basis. Each mortgage statement that is sent to the borrower monthly has payment options listed. The borrower can opt to pay the equivalent of a 30-year amortizing loan payment, an interest-only payment, or a graduated payment with potential deferred interest. This flexibility allows homeowners to make financial decisions each month on where they'd like to spend their money. If the borrower has another attractive investment option, it might make sense to pay as little as possible on the mortgage and invest the rest in stocks.

It takes the right buyer to understand and manage a deferred-interest loan, and this type of loan is not for everyone. But if it is carefully managed, this loan can provide long-term benefits to the client.

Assumable Loans

Some mortgage loans include a provision that allows the loan to be taken over, or the liability "assumed." The terms of the note can be carried over from one owner to another. For example, let's say that a seller puts his home on the market for $147,000 and the loan is assumable. The rate was 6 percent when he bought the home two years ago, and he owes $134,000 today.

Now let's say that if you were to take out a new mortgage loan today, the rate would be at 7.25 percent. If you have the money for the down payment on this loan, the $13,000, you have two options. You can either take the seller's loan or get a new one at today's higher rate. When the loan is assumable, you not only take over the interest rate. It means that you will need to pay the seller the difference between what the seller owes and what he asks for the home in down payment.

Not all loans can be assumed; only those containing an "assumption clause" are assumable. Usually, fixed-rate loans and their related products, such as a balloon loan, cannot be assumed. You more likely will find an ARM loan that is assumable.

The Lender's Role

The financing options are endless, and rather than take yourself down the wrong path or not know enough to take a left instead of a right, you must educate yourself through the experts. This is why it's imperative to find someone you like *and can understand* when choosing a lender. You've determined the monthly payment you're comfortable with. Based upon current market rates, you now know your maximum mortgage amount. Once you figure in the down payment, the lender can run scenarios on different loan solutions.

The question I always ask is, "How long can you envision yourself in this home?" or, at the very least, "How long can you see yourself in this mortgage?" If this is your first home, chances are you'll probably not be there for 30 years, and if you're not going to be there 30 years, do you need a 30-year loan? Sometimes the answer is yes, depending on your need for security. When you take on an ARM or balloon loan, it means that in a few years, if you want to stay in your home, you'll need to consider another financing solution. And we've said that no one yet has accurately read the future markets, so rates could be higher—or they may be lower. Some people cope with that idea well, while others can't sleep at night with that uncertainty. And again, you're the one with the checkbook, so you've got to determine where your comfort level lies.

You may never have all of the answers exactly right from the beginning, but taking time to plan what the loan means for you is crucial. It's different for everyone because no two sets of circumstances are the same. Keep that in mind as you get bombarded with advice from friends, family, and colleagues who have gone through the home-loan process before you. You cannot make a bad decision if you've done your homework and have chosen the loan based upon your situation, as you know it to be.

The Least You Need to Know

- "Fixed rate" means that the interest rate does not change, so the principal and interest payment you make stay the same for the term of the mortgage note.

- When shopping for adjustable-rate mortgage (ARM) loans, ask about the index (the money source the loan is adjusted in accordance with) and the margin (the lender's number on top of the index), which determine the maximum potential rate movement.

- Balloon mortgages are amortized like a fixed-rate loan, but usually the note is called due 5 or 7 years into the loan; rates are typically slightly lower than for a fixed-rate loan because of their shorter duration.

- ◆ Wonderful alternatives to fixed-rate financing exist, so explore all the options before thinking the fixed-rate loan is the only loan for you.

- ◆ Not all adjustable-rate loans have the same parameters. It's imperative that you discuss each loan program independently rather than assume that all ARM loans contain similar terms.

Chapter 10

Shopping for the Best Loan Package

In This Chapter

- ◆ Determining how much to put down
- ◆ Shopping for a rate versus shopping for a payment
- ◆ Buying discount points and buy-downs
- ◆ Coming up with creative solutions, such as no-PMI and combination loans

Money is a precious commodity because it affords us the things we want and need. But it's also—in most cases—hard to come by. Mortgage brokers across the country are finding that most prospective borrowers have fine jobs and decent credit, but have little to no money saved. So it's only natural to want the best value for your dollars. But how do you know what the best use of that savings is? Well, that's the subject of this chapter.

Understanding the Down Payment

In the early 1800s, it was not uncommon to need more than 50 percent for a down payment before a bank would consider you as a potential customer. It has never been easy to come up with that kind of savings, and, as a result, the government got involved with financing that could benefit more potential homebuyers. And today cash needed to purchase a home is considerably less than ever before. Let's learn the particulars.

A good place to start is with the amount of money you will need to put toward the purchase. The down payment is the difference between the price you pay for the home and the amount you need to borrow. For example, if you purchase a home for $161,600, a 10 percent down payment would be $16,160 ($161,600 × .10). The amount financed would then be $145,440 ($161,600 – $16,160).

We've already touched on the minimum down payment required for various kinds of loans, but here is a summary:

- On a conventional loan, the minimum down payment is generally 5 percent, although a few loan programs are available with 0 to 3 percent down. For almost all conventional mortgage loans, borrowers must be able to prove that they have a minimum of 5 percent of their own savings in the purchase, and then any additional cash can be gifted from a parent or relative.

- On an FHA loan, your total cash investment is a minimum of 3 percent, which is calculated on the sales price plus any allowable closing costs. And those monies can be your own savings, a gift, or a grant from a nonprofit group (more on this in the "No Down Payment?" section).

- On a VA loan, you are not required to have any down payment. If you do have cash to put into the purchase, the VA will reward you with a lower VA funding fee.

Understanding the Loan to Value

As you explore loan programs and rates, you'll find that a lot of answers hinge on how much money you intend to borrow in relation to the value of the home. This calculation is known as the *loan-to-value (LTV)* relationship.

def•i•ni•tion

The **loan-to-value (LTV)** is a relationship expressed as a ratio between the property value of the home and the amount of the loan.

We've been talking about the sales price up to this point, but it's really the value of the home that the lender is most concerned with. You can choose to pay whatever you like for a property, but the lender is willing to lend you money only based upon what he or she believes the home is worth. Another point to note here is that the lender bases everything off either the sales price or the appraised value, whichever is less.

To help you understand the LTV, let's say a home is valued at $200,000 and you've paid $198,000. You may have a 20 percent down payment, so, even though the home is worth $200,000, your offer to purchase was $198,000; your down payment is $198,000 × .20 = $39,600, leaving you with a loan amount of $158,400. Your loan-to-value is 80 percent ($158,400 ÷ $198,000), even though the value came in at $200,000. Remember, the lender calculates based upon whichever is less, sales price or appraised value.

What if, for the same house that you've offered to pay $198,000 for, the appraisal comes back to the lender at $195,000? You wanted a 20 percent down payment, but rather than calculate the 20 percent on the sales price, the lender will use the value in this case ($195,000 × .20 = $39,000). But now there's a dilemma because you have offered to pay $198,000, not $195,000. The lender will require you to come up with the additional $3,000, for a total of $42,000. Again, lenders lend based upon the lesser of the two, sales versus appraisal.

In the second example, you could either pay more for the home than its value and pay the additional $3,000 down, or you could put the $39,000 down, which is less than 20 percent and thus requires private mortgage insurance. You might also consider renegotiating with the seller to see if he or she is willing to reduce the price.

Here are some examples to reinforce the concept:

- If you have a 5 percent down payment, your LTV is 95 percent.

- If you have a 10 percent down payment, your LTV is 90 percent.

No Down Payment?

Can the LTV be 100 percent? At one time, not so very long ago, unless you were a veteran, it was unheard of for a borrower to buy a home without a down payment. Upon discovering you had no savings or gift monies available, the lender usually structured a savings plan to help you accumulate the sufficient amount of funds needed for a down payment.

Today several options are available to assist borrowers who have very little or no money to purchase a home. Mortgage-underwriting guidelines state that the seller cannot just give money to the buyer unless it's for a tangible item. But the guidelines go on to say that a buyer *can* accept money if it comes in the form of a gift or from a charitable source.

There are several organizations that will offer a seller-funded grant for the purpose of down payment. The way it works is the seller promises part of the their net proceeds of sale to the nonprofit group. The nonprofit organization acts as the conduit for the mere cost of the administrative fees, usually $500. This organization then offers a "gift" to the buyer to be used toward the down payment and/or closing costs for the home purchase. A few examples follow:

- **Nehemiah:** www.nehemiahcorp.org

- **Neighborhood Gold:** www.neighborhoodgold.com

- **Ameridream:** www.ameridreamcharity.org

- **Esther Foundation:** www.estherfoundation.org

All of these organizations have been established to provide an acceptable path by which a seller is able to transfer money from the sale of a home and get it to the buyer as a down payment. The key to this grant is the value of the property and the seller's ability to negotiate the price of the home and have enough left over to give to the buyer.

The grant doesn't work in all cases. For example, to fund a borrower's down payment on an FHA loan the seller would need to contribute 3 percent of the loan. The seller may not want to spend that much to sell the home, or he might not have enough equity to give. Equity is determined by the appraised value, and the property appraisal must support the sales price to make it work.

Up to this point, the only reason a seller would consider such a grant is to sell the house. If the buyer wants the house but has no money for down payment and the seller is in the position to give the down payment through the equity, giving such a grant makes sense. But to entice sellers to participate in these programs, the Esther Foundation has taken the grant process one step further and has registered as a charitable organization. This gives it the right to allow the funds that come through its system to be treated as a charitable contribution from seller to buyer. Therefore, not only is the seller selling the home by using this resource, but he or she has a tax write-off, to boot. This is a new twist, so expect to see other organizations follow suit.

Local community initiatives also give buyer assistance. The Community Reinvestment Act (CRA) requires banks to give back to the communities that they do business in. So many of the banks choose to offer low- to moderate-income home loans for little to no out-of-pocket money. And neighborhood-revitalization groups offer assistance to entice potential homeowners to buy homes in economically distressed areas. Money may be available to purchase a home or for home improvements later. As an example, one community sells a property by lottery for $1. The buyer is then required to invest a certain amount of labor and resources into the property for improvements.

Fannie Mae and Freddie Mac also allow 100 percent financing for borrowers that meet specific income and credit score requirements. Many of these programs also offer expanded qualification guidelines to allow more people to qualify. The interest rates can be higher, but it may make sense to consider these types of loans if it means that you can buy a home today.

The Rate vs. Payment

I caution you against shopping for a loan based solely on the lowest rate. You may fall prey to misleading advertisers that hope to lure you in. It has been our experience that the borrower who focuses only on the interest rate is missing the bigger picture. Remember, it's not the interest rate you pay monthly; it's a house payment. The house payment is what needs to fit into your monthly budget. And although the rate is important in calculating the house payment, it is not the only factor. Interest rates cost money. The savvy shopper understands the relationship between the rate and the cost of the rate.

Discount Points and the Permanent-Rate Buy-Down

Be cautious of lenders who talk only about their rates. Interest rates are available on a sliding scale. A rate is available that will not cost you extra money, and that rate also may be lowered if you're willing to pay some additional up-front fees. Said another way, the lower the interest rate, the higher the cost to obtain the rate. This practice is called "discounting" the interest rate. And, frankly, discounting the rate often makes no sense to the borrower.

To illustrate, let's say today's true market interest rate, or "par rate," is 6.50 percent. The par rate means there are no added fees to get that particular rate. But you don't want to pay 6.50 percent; you'd like a lower rate because lower is perceived as a better value (and maybe your neighbor got that rate a month ago). The lender might perhaps offer you a 6.25 percent rate but ask you to pay an up-front fee, and, in return, provide you a lower rate for the term of your loan. The money paid up front is considered as paying *discount points*. In dollars, 1 discount point equals 1 percent of the loan amount; a rule of thumb is 1 point for each ⅛ to ¼ drop in the interest rate. This relationship will vary based on market conditions.

def•i•ni•tion

A **discount point** is the cost associated with purchasing a lower interest rate than the prevailing market; it is considered prepaid interest.

For example, on a $145,400 loan (30-year term) with a par rate of 6.5 percent, here are the calculations:

Payment at 6.5% is $918.93, no points

Your new rate: 6.25 = (6.5 − 0.25)

Payment at 6.25% is $895.67, for 1 point or $1,454.00

Your monthly payment savings—principal and interest: $23.26 = ($918.93 − $895.67)

Your recoup period: 62.51 months = ($1,454.00 ÷ $23.26)

Basically, you would need to stay in the home longer than 63 months (more than 5 years) to recoup the cost of the discount points you paid.

Here is a snapshot view of how interest rates may be priced on any given day. The concept to grasp here is that the lender truly does not care which rate combination you choose because the net effect is the same. In other words, each of these rate scenarios gives the lender the same return. But you as a borrower may find that one will suit your purpose better than another.

The following table also illustrates how rates may vary based upon how long you might need the interest rate to be guaranteed, or locked in from application to loan closing. As the number of days until the loan closes increases, so does the cost of the rate. Each point is calculated as a percentage of the loan amount. Usually, your purchase agreement will dictate the timeline in which the transaction must be performed, hence how long the rate lock must be in place.

Interest-Rate Comparison–30-Year Fixed Rate

Rate	15 Days	30 Days	60 Days
5.500	1.25 points	1.75 points	2.00 points
5.625	0.75 points	1.25 points	1.50 points
5.750	0.25 points	0.50 points	0.75 points
5.875	(0.25) points*	0.00 points	0.25 points
6.000	(0.75) points*	(0.25) points*	0.00 points
6.125	(1.50) points*	(1.00) points*	(0.75) points

Denotes the point at which the lender will actually pay you money for taking that rate. The lender will usually offer to pay closing-cost expenses. These monies cannot be used for the down payment.

Rates can be locked in for as many as 360 days, but typically the lender will charge an extended lock-in fee. Because there is no way to predict future market conditions, the up-front fee hedges the lender's risk somewhat. Usually, there is no additional expense for transactions completed within 60 days.

If you are negotiating with the seller on the sales price, you can try to include the cost of any discount points to buy down the rate. The seller probably will not negotiate as much on the price you pay, but you will build the cost of obtaining the rate into your loan. And work through the numbers: it might make sense to pay a bit more for the house for the advantage of having to pay less money at closing or getting a lower interest rate.

This is the "pay me now or pay me later" philosophy of borrowing money. If you decide to pay extra today, your rate will be lower, but if you don't want to pay extra, your rate will be higher. And just because you're paying a lower interest rate doesn't mean that's a better loan. You've seen the impact of paying points, both monthly and as closing costs. You've also seen the monthly savings after paying to discount the rate. A tool financial planners use to evaluate the best way to go is a calculation called present value. Present value simply means to take into account the cost of doing business at today's price.

Discount points take time—in most cases, years—to recover. Ideally, when a borrower pays points up front to discount the interest rate, he or she should expect to be in the home long enough to recover the initial cash investment. The monthly savings experienced, then, is worthwhile. Otherwise, those dollars paid up front benefit only the lender. So just because the rate is lower, it doesn't mean that you're spending less money. That's why shopping for a rate may not always give you the best results. Remember, it's the total cost of the loan that is important.

The Temporary Buy-Down

We've reviewed how you can pay discount points at closing to get a lower interest rate permanently on a mortgage loan. But a loan rate can also be brought down temporarily. A third party to the transaction, such as the seller or builder, can pay money at closing that covers a portion of the borrower's mortgage payment. The amount they pay is the difference between the rate they've advertised and the actual note rate. So the borrower pays less monthly than what their note indicates. The buyer wins because their house payment is low, and the seller wins because they've been able to create a financing package that sells the house. And there's no added overall expense to the seller because he or she will recover the expense of the temporary buy-down through the sales price of the home.

The interest rate will increase gradually every 6 to 12 months (depending upon how the plan was set up) until it reaches the note rate. The following typical buy-down is called a 2–1 buy-down and has a 30-year term. The loan program gets its name because the interest rate the borrower pays in the beginning is 2 percent below the actual note rate the first year. The rate moves up to 1 percent below the note rate the second year, and increases to the note rate for the third to thirtieth years.

Suppose we have a 2-1 buy-down with a note rate of 6 percent. Our first year the rate is going to be 4 percent, the second year it rises to 5 percent, and the third through thirtieth year it is 6 percent. The lender is still getting the full 6 percent interest each year, but the seller picks up the difference during the first two years. It's not until the third year, when the seller's buy-down amount runs out, that we are asked to pay the actual payment due for the 6 percent interest rate we agreed upon with the lender.

Here's what it looks like for a mortgage of $145,400:

Year	Rate	Borrower pays	Seller pays	Annual subsidy
1	4%	$693.56	$178.84	$2,146.08
2	5%	$780.80	$91.60	$1,099.20
3–30	6%	$872.40	$00.00	$00.00
Total seller buy-down				$3,245.28

The builder or seller did not offer this financing for free. More likely, he or she added the $3,245.28 (cost of financing the buy-down) to the sales price of the home, which then means that you have more than likely financed the cost of the buy-down over the loan term.

Is this a bad deal? Certainly not, if you consider the monthly savings and also keep the home a number of years to allow the home's appreciation and your equity build-up to catch up with the $3,245.28 used as a financing concession.

PMI/MIP: Is There Another Way?

Mortgage insurance coverage has enabled lenders to loosen up on their restrictions over the years. By allowing homeowners to purchase with as little as 5 percent down payment, the industry opened up home ownership to a tremendous number of new buyers. But many borrowers have voiced loud objections at how expensive the insurance can sometimes be and the fact that it's paid by the borrower but yet gives no direct benefit or protection to them.

Until recently, it was impossible to get a loan with less than a 20 percent down payment without PMI. And the FHA, as we said, always requires the insurance. But the lending community listened, and today there are a couple of other solutions to explore:

◆ No-PMI loans

◆ Combination first and second mortgages

No-PMI Loans

Many borrowers complain about how expensive PMI is. In response, the industry has created a way to bypass the monthly insurance premium. The names may vary a bit from company to company, so as you shop for lenders, ask about no-PMI loans or loans with lender-paid mortgage insurance, LPMI loans.

You should find that with as little as 5 percent down, you can avoid the mortgage insurance if you're willing to accept a slightly higher interest rate. In order to pull off the higher rate, the mortgage industry keeps the interest rate just below what the PMI premium rates are. The interest rate is typically higher because the risk to the lender is greater without the insurance. (So you are paying for the risk via a higher interest rate, but it is tax-deductible.)

Why would anyone take a higher interest rate over a lower rate? Because if you compare the two loans side by side, without the escrow monthly mortgage insurance, the overall housing expense is lower. But how could that be, you ask? Because the lending industry became very smart and realized that there probably wasn't as much risk to these higher LTV loans as what they had thought years ago. They also realized that by self-insuring the loans, they were able to create another profitable series of loans because they could charge more for the higher risk. And not only is your payment lower, but because you've increased your interest rate, your tax-deductible interest has also increased.

First/Second Combination Loans (80/10/10) (80/15/5) (80/20)

In recent years, second mortgages have been all the rage. It seems lots of homebuyers have taken full advantage of their equity by securing home equity loans and lines of credit. We discuss these loans as they pertain to refinancing in Chapter 13, but they can also be helpful in avoiding the mortgage insurance when you are purchasing a home.

Most underwriting guidelines have always stated that it is fine for a borrower to secure a second mortgage loan against the savings (equity) in the home, as long as the lender's lien was kept in first position. Historically, the buyer has always asked the seller to provide them with a second mortgage, either to help with the down payment or keep the payment low enough to qualify.

Today it is quite common to use a second mortgage in order to avoid PMI. Here's how it works. Let's say you have a 10 percent down payment available to put toward your home purchase. Consider taking a second loan for the additional 10 percent; the total down payment is now 20 percent and you no longer need mortgage insurance. The same works with a 5 percent down payment and a second mortgage of 15 percent. And if you have no money for a down payment, consider an 80/20 combination that allows you to borrow the full 20 percent.

The second mortgage can be repaid as an interest-only line of credit—or as an installment loan with a fixed payment. Because the second loan is a mortgage, there is the additional tax deduction in most cases, which makes this option more attractive than the loans with PMI.

Before You Sign

As of this writing, PMI has no tax benefit, but that might change. Always check with your tax advisor on deductions to make sure you have the most up-to-date information.

The following comparison will help you understand your options as you try to decide whether you want a loan with PMI. Note that the rate is usually lower on the *home-equity line of credit* (*HELOC*) than on the *home equity loan* because, as with first mortgages, the lender will usually charge a higher interest rate on a longer-term loan.

def•i•ni•tion

A **home equity loan** is an installment loan that requires the loan against the savings in the home to be repaid in equal installments for a specified period of time, with definite beginning and ending dates. A **home equity line of credit (HELOC)** is a revolving loan usually associated with the prime rate, which enables the homeowners to use their home's equity as collateral on a loan. Payments are normally calculated with minimum interest only and no required principal reduction, usually available for up to 10 years.

Comparing Your Mortgage Insurance Options

Let's say you have less than 20 percent to put down on your home, and you're not interested in having two mortgages. Here is a comparison of your options:

♦ Traditional financing with PMI

Example: Sales price of $161,600 with 10 percent down = $16,200 down payment

Total mortgage amount: $145,400 @ 6 percent interest rate. P&I = $871.75 + $65.00 (per month PMI) = $936.75

♦ No-PMI financing

It's Your Money

As mentioned earlier, the second mortgage can be on a fixed payment or can be a HELOC with a flexible rate, interest only. For comparisons, this example is the lesser of the two payments, interest only. The home equity loan would be higher monthly, making the payment comparable to the no-PMI payment.

Example: Sales price of $161,600 with 10 percent down = $16,200 down payment

Total mortgage amount: $145,400 @ 6.5 percent interest rate (higher rate) = $918.93 (no PMI needed)

♦ First/second combination loans

Example: (80/10/10) Sales price of $161,600 with 20 percent down = $32,320 down payment (10 percent cash and another 10 percent in a second mortgage)

First mortgage $129,250 @ 6 percent rate = $775.60

Second mortgage $16,200 @ 7 percent (prime rate) = $93.21

Total mortgage amount: first mortgage ($775.60) + second mortgage ($83.22) = $868.81

Each of these loan solutions accomplishes the purchase, but with different characteristics. The traditional method shows the payment plus PMI at $936.75, the no-PMI option shows the payment of $918.93, and the combination loan assumes $858.85.

Here are a few ideas to consider when making your comparison:

♦ How long will you be in the home? Mortgage insurance can eventually be removed. Do you really need to pay the higher interest rate or take a second mortgage? Check with your lender first regarding the criteria for removing mortgage insurance. Usually, PMI can be removed within 12 to 24 months. For an FHA loan, when the loan balance is reduced to 78 percent of the original sales price or appraised value, the insurance is no longer required. The FHA's monthly insurance payment must be paid for a minimum of five years.

♦ Are you on a fixed budget? The predictability of the mortgage payment may be important. The lender-paid mortgage insurance may work well.

♦ Will you prepay this loan? If yes, you may like the first/second mortgage option because you could eliminate the second mortgage and eventually have only the first one without the monthly insurance cost.

♦ Is no mortgage insurance available? Not every lender offers it, and those that do may offer it only on specific products.

♦ Are additional costs associated with any of these options? Aside from the hike in interest rates on lender-paid mortgage insurance, there should be no additional extras.

Remember also that the average life expectancy of a mortgage is five to seven years, so it's possible that you would be in a position to refinance no matter which loan you start with.

The Least You Need to Know

- The cash available to purchase and the source of the down payment often dictate the mortgage solution best suited for you.

- The lower rate may not always be the best deal for a borrower; reserve judgment until you take into consideration the cost of the rate and determine the payback years of that rate in relation to the money it costs to obtain the rate.

- A temporary interest rate buy-down is typically offered by the seller or builder to create foot traffic through a property; the cost of the lower initial interest rate is most often built into the cost of the home.

- Several different solutions are available on a conventional loan regarding mortgage insurance. It's prudent to review your options with the lender to determine which may be the best for your long-term objectives.

Chapter **11**

Shopping for the Perfect Home

In This Chapter

- ◆ Looking with and without a real estate agent
- ◆ Getting the right inspections and appraisals
- ◆ Making sense of different types of properties
- ◆ Mortgaging a home you have built

You know your price range, and you are knowledgeable about loan programs. You have an idea of what fees and the monthly payment are because you've completed your qualification with the lender (in Chapter 4). Now comes the fun ... looking at homes. Finally, you're about to make all of this preparation seem real.

The property you choose plays a large part in the type of mortgage you need. Not all homes are financed the same way. For example, not all condominiums can be financed on a conforming loan. And a home under construction requires different considerations than an existing dwelling.

It may be the home you choose that dictates the financing you need.

Looking on Your Own and the Internet

Driving neighborhoods on Sunday has become a pastime for many of us. We drive the streets admiring the homes and their architecture and gardens. We may daydream about adding a porch, or what our car would look like in the driveway. Many homes, if for sale, may be available for an open house preview. Most of us choose to look at the homes that appeal to us aesthetically.

At the end of the day, we may have seen a lot of homes that we've enjoyed, but perhaps not one met our needs. After all, looking at homes is only a hobby.

It's Your Money

Pay attention not only to the sales price of the home, but also to the real estate property taxes. As you shop for neighborhoods, note the differences in the tax rate. Adjoining communities may have very different rates, which could dramatically impact your monthly payment.

Please don't mistake this process for house hunting. Looking for a home should be done in a systematic manner. The preview process is helpful and can even be fun as you're trying to narrow your search to specific neighborhoods and home styles. But once you've settled down and understand the market, it's time to organize your needs versus your wants.

Each community has its own micro market. A home that is marketed at $125,000 on the east side of town may be totally different than the same-priced home on the north side of the city. By previewing neighborhoods, you'll get a feel for how home size relates to price and which community may have homes that fit both your needs and your price range.

It's Your Money

Websites that may help you get a feel for what's being listed include Realtor.com and Homeagain.com.

But driving around and hoping you come across a home that meets your criteria is like looking for the needle in the haystack. Fortunately, we have resources such as the Internet, which literally puts information at our fingertips. What once took days to uncover in research now can be done in a fraction of the time.

Many websites assist you in locating homes that are for sale. Most have details on square footage, number of beds and baths, property taxes, and school districts. You can also easily find what houses have sold for in the neighborhoods you're interested in and that meet your price criteria. If you're working on your own, you then contact the appropriate party to preview the home.

The Realtor's Role

The term "Realtor" is a registered trademark that can be used by any real estate agent who is a member of the National Association of Realtors. Real estate agents have traditionally been the primary resource for borrowers when it comes to locating and purchasing real estate because they know their market. Realtors have up-to-the-minute data if they are part of their real estate board's Multiple Listing Service (MLS). The MLS provides them with both printed and online information about the goings-on: what has sold, when, how much, and what's available and new. And when you're looking, they can tell you when properties meeting your criteria come on the market for sale.

Because they're professionals, they want to do the best job for you. So most Realtors will want to know that you are preapproved and for what kind of loan. That helps them to know your price range and whether you need any special financing assistance from the seller as you negotiate. The real estate professional's job is to help you locate the home that meets your needs at the price you can afford.

Before You Sign _____

You can hire a real estate agent to represent your interests in a home purchase. As your buyer's agent, this agent then can give you information on comparable homes and pricing, and offer you insight on making an offer. The agent's fee is negotiated and paid by either you or a willing seller. Remember, if an agent doesn't represent you, his or her loyalty is with the seller.

Your agent can offer objective insight into the purchase and perhaps help determine whether the home will meet your long-term objective. For instance, suppose you find the perfect lot with the not-so-perfect home. A real estate agent can help you decide whether it makes sense to buy the house and remodel it. It might be the case that you "over-improve" the house for the market, making it difficult for resale later. These are the kinds of issues that real estate agents can research and advise buyers on.

And if you like the home and want to make an offer, the agent will also draft the purchase contract and present it to the seller's agent. The agent not only assists with the home selection, but most agents will also provide you with reliable contacts for termite inspections, home inspections, and even the name of a lender if you still need a recommendation. And they're with you through the loan closing as your liaison in the transaction.

Keep in mind that there are some regional differences in the services provided by real estate agents. For example, on the East Coast the Realtor works in conjunction with an attorney to finalize the contract negotiations. A Realtor's negotiation and closing involvement might be restricted because of the legal representation and precedent already in place.

For Sale by Owner (FSBO)

Technology has allowed homebuyers to market homes through the Internet. With sophisticated programs and websites established for broad distribution, homeowners can now price and market their own home. The incentive to homeowners is that they avoid paying a real estate commission, or transaction fee, due upon sale and closing. The seller is responsible for the cost to sell the home traditionally, and the fee is split between the buyer's agent and the agent representing the seller.

Without the added expense to the seller to sell the home, the buyer theoretically should get a better price on the home.

But without some market knowledge, the buyer will find it hard to determine whether there is really a savings to buy direct rather than through a Realtor. Some FSBOs (pronounced "fizzbo") will negotiate their sale with a Realtor who might represent a buyer even though they've chosen not to have themselves represented. That agent's fee would need to be negotiated as part of the purchase. If the seller does not want to transact with a Realtor, the fee would then be your expense.

Disadvantages to buying a home for sale by owner are that you're not given as much information from a seller as a Realtor representing you might provide. Also, without a Realtor, the buyer and seller both are responsible for all of the details of the transaction, from arranging inspections to coordinating the loan closing. For the experienced buyer, the process may not be so foreign, although it's still time-consuming. But for the first-time buyer, the tasks can be overwhelming, not to mention unnerving.

Financing a home purchase remains the same regardless of whether you work with a Realtor or directly with the seller. But without a professional real estate agent's advice and insight, you risk making an offer on property that won't meet the lender's property requirement for your loan choice, or even offering too much for the home because you don't have all of the neighborhood comparables an agent will usually provide.

Realtors are market professionals. Their job is to know the real estate in your area. Most good Realtors will educate you and offer service from the initial stages through the closing.

Negotiating for the Home

After you've located a home, you then begin the process of negotiating for its purchase. You prepare an offer to purchase, which includes not only the price you are willing to pay, but any terms and conditions. For a preapproved borrower, this process should be easy because you've already rehearsed the numbers before arriving at this point. You'll be making an offer of price, and you'll be asking for consideration of your price based upon stipulations, or contingencies.

The contingencies are put into the language to allow you time to take care of business with regards to your offer. You may love the home but question the condition of the roof and water heater. Rather than take the chance that someone else will come in to make an offer on the home, the buyer "seals the deal" contingent upon an inspection to verify the condition of the roof and water heater. Here are some typical contingencies that a Realtor will place in the contract to protect the interest of both parties:

- ◆ **Contingent on buyer's ability to obtain suitable financing.** This gives the buyer time to explore financing options.

- ◆ **Contingent on buyer's lender to provide satisfactory opinion letter.** This permits the buyer to verify their ability to purchase.

- ◆ **Contingent on seller's ability to find suitable housing.** This gives a potential seller time to find a place to live before completing the sale of their home.

- ◆ **Contingent on attorney review of the terms and conditions of the contract.** This gives either party the time to have the contract reviewed by an attorney.

- ◆ **Contingent on a satisfactory home inspection to verify the condition of the home.** This contingency allows the buyer to have the home inspected.

- ◆ **Contingent on sale closing of previous home.** This allows buyers to use proceeds from the sale of their existing home toward down payment and closing expenses of the new home.

Contingencies are written into the contract with a time limitation attached, usually a couple of days to a couple of weeks, depending upon the type of contingency.

When buyer and seller negotiate, the seller has a price in mind that he may be willing to negotiate to, and the buyer knows what he is willing to pay. If the buyer needs funds to offset some expenses, he can ask the seller for funds to cover closing costs and/or prepaid costs, but not the down payment. Why would the seller consider giving the buyer money to close, when closing may cost $1,500 to $2,500?

Let's assume that the sales price of the home the seller is offering is $140,000, but in his mind, he knows he'd sell for $137,000. And let's assume that the borrower senses the seller's price and offers $139,000, and asks the seller to cover the closing costs also for $2,000. To the seller the net is the same.

$139,000

−2,000

$137,000

The seller is able to sell and net his price. The buyer has paid $2,000 more for the home, but he receives the extra dollars to use toward closing costs. For every $1,000 the price is adjusted, it's an extra $6 to 8 per month. The cost versus rate must be analyzed, but it may be the only way the buyer would have enough money to close.

When you've agreed upon the price, you sign the agreement and offer an *earnest money* deposit. In good faith, you pledge to the seller that if they accept your offer, you'll provide them with a deposit, held by the Realtor or third party. The offer may go back and forth between the parties a couple of times to fine-tune the terms. And if the buyer and seller come to an agreement, the contract is executed by all parties and the sale is consummated.

def•i•ni•tion

Earnest money is good-faith money deposited with a third party to reinforce the borrower's intention to purchase.

With your knowledge of financing and the lender's approval letter, the home negotiations should proceed. But don't be alarmed if the process seems less than comfortable. After all, you're probably buying your most expensive thing to date, and the seller is probably just as concerned about selling the asset. And in any transaction involving money, tensions and emotions can rise.

Inspections

As part of the agreement to purchase, there are usually contingencies that relate to third-party inspections of the home. Some are built into the contract based upon regional requirements, such as a termite report. Others are the borrower's preference. The buyer may request a home inspection to independently review and assess the condition of the home. The inspector will thoroughly examine the mechanical and structural components of the home, and determine any immediate or long-range maintenance and repair items. The comprehensive inspection either reinforces the prospective buyer's position to purchase or leads to another round of negotiation to remedy the deficiencies. In some cases, there are irreconcilable differences, and both parties will part ways.

The Appraisal

When the offer is accepted and all inspections have been dealt with, the lender orders an appraisal of the home. The property appraisal is again performed by an independent contractor, who walks through the home to decide its market value. In this case, however, the appraiser is not looking as closely at the mechanical or structural integrity of the home. Instead, the focus is to determine the makeup of the home and compare it to other similar homes that have sold in the area within the last six months.

The home's appraisal is the most important document in the transaction because the lender wants to make absolutely sure that the money he or she is lending on this home will have adequate collateral. If the buyer cannot fulfill the contractual obligation to repay the note, the lender may need to take back the home, in which case the lender needs to know that it can be resold to recover the lender's cash investment.

The home appraisal should therefore never be considered a substitute for the home inspection. The two inspections are done for two totally different purposes.

Understanding Appraisal Valuations

The property appraisal is done based upon historic data. In theory, a home is worth only what someone is willing to pay for it. But there must be a baseline to start the pricing. The appraiser sets out to find three properties within a 1-mile radius of the home that fits the description of the subject. The appraiser checks closed loan data because a home's value is what someone will pay. If you look in past records, what someone else has been willing to pay for a similar house offers a starting place for pricing the next house.

It's rare to find three homes with identical features in the same condition in the neighborhood that have recently sold. So the appraiser looks for comparable housing and adjusts the model as needed. For example, if the subject home is a three-bedroom, one-and-a-half-bath, two-story home with a two-car garage, the appraiser will look for a similar home that recently sold. Once or twice he may find the same style but different ages or conditions. He may also need to pull into the mix a four-bedroom, two-bath home and adjust for the difference in size, features, and marketability.

It may be also that the market the home is located in will require a larger scope of review—farther than the 1-mile radius. In the foothills outside of Denver, for example, it's not unusual to have an appraiser use a comparable from several miles away, primarily because of the distance between homes. Again, the appraiser is using what data is available to determine fair market value for the real estate.

The value of the home increases based upon the demands for housing in the area, inflation, and the costs to reproduce the home. This is called appreciation, or a positive gain on your investment. Over time, it seems that the cost/value of everything goes up—remember the stories about when a loaf of bread was 5¢? And although it's helpful to know what the previous owners paid for the home when they bought it, that price is only a starting place in setting the current value.

The appraisal is the document that verifies that the home is worth what the seller is asking. The lender must verify that the property is good collateral for the loan. You also benefit from this process because this is a real estate investment as well as your home. And as an investment, you want to know that it's worth what you're paying for it. Then as a homeowner, you can keep track of your asset's growth, through principal reduction and market appreciation.

Condominiums and Multifamily Homes

Up to this point, the term *home* has been used in general terms. Yet there are different types of housing available. And there can be differences in how the financing is handled for each type.

Condominiums are popping up in communities from coast to coast. Condo living has always been very practical in urban settings, but their popularity has soared in the last five years, partially due to the baby boomer generation downsizing. When you buy a condo, you are attached to a group and become part of a mini community. Your dwelling is immediately affected by how well your project is managed and how well the complex is maintained.

A condo project typically has an association that manages the maintenance and upkeep of the entire complex. The condominium project and the individual unit you're interested in must be reviewed and approved by the lender. The lender will make certain that the project is well managed. Lenders like to see the ratio of owner-occupied units to rental units and understand what, if any, future annexation is planned. And in the case of FHA and VA financing, they may also need to review the construction type before allowing units to be financed with their products. If you're considering a condo, let the lender know. When qualifying you, lenders need to take into account the home-owner's association dues monthly. The dues cover the dwelling insurance and the cost of maintenance and upkeep. And although these fees are not escrowed, they are an expense and must be included in the overall calculation and underwriting review.

A multifamily home is considered attached housing of two to four units. If you're looking at your home purchase as an investment, it's a perk to have another unit or two that you can rent and earn income on to offset your housing expense. Of course, there are considerations before entering into this type of investment, including multiple maintenance issues, what happens if there's a vacancy, availability of cash reserves to cover extra costs, and so on.

The lender brings all of the aforementioned issues to the table during the qualification process. For multifamily housing, the down payment requirement is usually a minimum of 10 percent, with the exception of an FHA loan, which still allows you a minimum cash investment on two-unit dwellings. They want to know that you will be occupying one unit because the interest rate is different for a true investment loan classified as a non-owner-occupied property. The FHA no longer offers loans on investment homes. The risk is higher to the lender because there are unknown variables, such as how the market may tolerate the rental, so things change a little. The appraisal is more expensive to generate because the appraiser must address the rental market in the report. The lender also will ask to see cash reserves, or money left in the bank after closing. The lender may also ask you for evidence that you are qualified to manage real estate. Again, if you are considering a property with multiple units, it is important to let the lender know. Your lender can then walk you through your options so there aren't any surprises later.

Second Homes and Vacation Properties

Once you own one home, you might be inclined to own more. We discuss real estate as an investment strategy next, but suppose you want to own more than one home for merely your own personal use. Is it possible? Sure it is, and lenders have made it relatively easy to do. It may be a place your family visits each year for vacations, or your children might live on the West Coast and you in the East. It has even become popular to have a home on a little lake an hour away.

The qualification guidelines are very similar to those for owner-occupied dwellings. The down payment requirements and interest rates stay the same as long as you can establish that the new home is farther than 75 miles from your primary residence and determine what draws you to the home regularly. The guides say you must occupy this property for a minimum of two weeks per year for it to qualify as a second home. You will need to qualify for both properties, and most lenders will not allow you to use gift funds for the purchase; you must be able to show your own funds.

The lender's objective is to make certain you don't intend to use the home as a full-time rental because those guidelines are different.

Investment Property

If you are interested in starting a career in the footsteps of Donald Trump, real estate is a fine way to diversify your investment portfolio. Again, there are differences in financing, such as a higher down payment—usually 10 to 20 percent. Depending on the number of units and your credit rating, you may find the opportunity for no money down. But lenders today offering 100% investment financing are offsetting the risk with higher rates, and that may affect your cash flow and income potential. Rental income on the units may be considered to offset the payment and help you to qualify. Expect the lender to allow up to 75 percent of the gross rents.

Some lenders will do investment loans only with an adjustable-rate loan. Interest rates are usually one-half of a percent higher than owner-occupied rates. If you are buying your first investment property, you may be asked to provide information on why you think you can manage real estate. Perhaps you work in a home maintenance–related field, or you have had money-management experience that could be applied to rentals.

Some lenders handle only owner-occupied purchases, so ask the right questions as you shop lenders. Mortgage companies typically handle loans for property with up to four units. If there are more than four units, the building is considered commercial, and different financing solutions (and lenders) apply.

Lot Loans

Most lenders will tell you that they are in the business of securing their loans with improved real estate. In other words, their loan is based upon the house, not the land it sits on. Some mortgage companies do provide lot loans, but it's not their primary business. They usually offer the loan assuming a house will be built on the lot. A lender will consider lending and will expect to review plans and specifications outlining how the home will be constructed on the land within 12 months of the purchase.

Interest is usually charged on a lot loan at prime rate plus a margin of profit determined by the lending institution. Down payment requirements vary, but 10 to 20 percent is typical. The lot is considered as equity when calculating the loan-to-value for the purpose of the construction and end loan financing, so any money put toward the lot carries through.

Some lenders will provide a loan on a lot knowing that it's not going to be improved. In most of these cases, the lender knows he's not going to be getting a great deal of return, so he'll likely ask for a larger down payment, such as 20 to 25 percent, before lending you the money.

New Construction

We cannot forget the home that's not yet a home. No mortgage loan guide would be complete without information on new construction. The term *new construction* applies to a home that has yet to be started, up through a home that has been recently built but not yet lived in. Again, there are different financing considerations, depending upon which phase you happen to be in.

When you build, there are two phases to the process: the actual construction (excavating, digging the hole, and erecting the structure) and the completed home. There are two loans, the construction loan and "the end loan," or mortgage loan. Depending on the agreement you have with the builder, you may be responsible for obtaining one or both. The builder usually needs financing to build your home. The builder may have a line of credit established or may have expertise only in building, not financing, in which case you would need to explore another loan type. As you may have already guessed, you must understand and meet certain criteria when you decide to finance a new build.

The end loan is the same as what you've already learned about, except that because it takes a while to build (anywhere from 4 to 12 months, depending upon the builder), there could be a difference in how long the loan rate can be locked. You'll need to review the lock options available through your lender. But the construction loan is different. Because there are now two parties involved, the lender will want to see the builder's credentials, credit, plans and specifications for the home, construction schedule, information on the lot, information on who owns it (you or the builder), and perhaps even references.

A construction loan is usually a line of credit, and the money is made available as the work is completed. For example, it may take one month to excavate, dig, set the foundation, and pour the basement. And that may cost $20,000. The lender would inspect the work and advance the money. At that point, the payments begin on the $20,000 advance, usually interest only. The construction continues, with usually three to four draws. The loan balance rises accordingly. The payments also go up as the draws go up. When the home is built, a final inspection is done to verify that the home has been completed according to the plans and project specifications that were originally approved. If the builder has taken out the loan, a lot of this takes place without you being aware of it. You may or may not realize that the builder has incorporated the loan cost into the price of the home.

Some lenders specialize in the combination of construction and end loan. The construction loan experts will offer you a loan package that automatically rolls the construction loan into the final mortgage loan. You can expect extra fees, but this type of loan is becoming more common, so you should expect perhaps 1 to 2 percent of sales price at most in additional costs. And the price is typically worth it to have the home of your dreams.

If you find a home offered for build by a production builder, the builder may have a financing package available as part of the promotion to buy. Read the fine print to see if you must use the builder's lender or if you can choose your own and carry over the promotional offer. Remember again that the low, enticing rate the builder is offering is often temporary and that the cost of the financing has been built into the sales price of the home. In other words, you're paying more for the home because of the perks the builder has paid on your behalf as part of the financing. This is a problem only if you need to resell unexpectedly in the next few years because you may not have as much equity built up. Review the section on temporary buy-down loans from Chapter 10, because these are popular marketing tools for the builder.

Now, pay close attention. This issue is where a lot of homebuyers get caught. If the builder has offered a temporary interest rate buy-down that you are taking advantage of, you must understand what happens to the payment at each adjustment. You should fully understand what a temporary buy-down is and how it moves. If you do not completely understand, revisit this point with the lender. Not only will the interest rate adjust upward, but the property taxes also will be adjusted upward. The lot is taxed as land only until the home is sold. Once the home has sold, the improved land value will obviously be higher. The tax office will reassess the lot with the completed home within 6 to 12 months of the closing and adjust the taxes accordingly.

On new construction, the property tax amount at the loan closing will reflect the assessment based upon unimproved land. You should be offered the opportunity to include the actual tax amount (based upon only the lot value until after the home is sold) or an estimate of what the taxes should be. Weigh this option carefully. I have had more than one call from a borrower 12 months after a new build closing, asking me to help figure out how the borrower can afford the increased payments he had not properly anticipated due to the temporary interest rate buy-down and the tax increase.

Manufactured Housing and Log Homes

Other types of housing also require special consideration with the mortgage. The term *manufactured* refers to modular homes, homes with log construction, and earth dome homes. Because the structure, and not the land, insures the lender's security position for the loan, you may find that you don't have as many loan options to choose from when you purchase this type of home.

For example, the VA allows 100 percent financing, with a few exceptions. However, when purchasing manufactured housing, it requires a minimum 10 percent down payment. If you are interested in purchasing land for a single- or double-wide mobile home, it's possible to get a loan, but all guidelines state that the vehicle must have a permanent foundation in place, must have no means of mobility once placed, and must be considered personal property.

The appraisal stipulations stay the same: the lender must be able to identify three similar properties within a reasonable distance of the subject to support the value and practicality of the loan.

Timeshares, Condotels, and Cooperatives

A timeshare is a single unit that has multiple owners. Mortgage companies traditionally do not lend on these homes because if the client defaults on the loan, the property cannot be taken back because of the other owners. Timeshare financing is usually offered by private financers or banks that have agreed to take on the loan without the mortgage as security.

A condotel is a property usually found in a resort or vacation community that is put into the rental pool of the resort for bookings. Condotels usually have a front desk and have rental practices more like those of a hotel. A rule of thumb for a mortgage company to consider a loan is whether the property can be leased out on a daily basis. Condotels can be financed, but they require special consideration. Usually these loans are handled by portfolio lenders.

Cooperatives are properties that function like a condo, except that you own a share of the corporation that owns the building your unit is in; you then "lease" the property from the corporation. In other words, you do not own the dwelling you occupy. Again, you'll find that your choices may be limited, but in this case, local financing is usually a sure thing. In New York City, for example, co-ops are everywhere, and the local lenders are very familiar with where to send the loans.

Have fun looking at houses. There are a variety of styles and shapes to choose from. Consider each house you preview one step closer to your home. And the old adage "You'll know it when you see it" cannot be truer than here. Somehow the houses we are supposed to have wait until we arrive.

The Least You Need to Know

- ◆ A real estate agent can help you identify properties that may meet your criteria by searching their Multiple Listing Service (MLS) network.

- ◆ The type of property you choose may directly influence the loan product, down payment, and interest rate you end up with.

- ◆ The property appraisal is done to assure the buyer that the home is worth what they're paying and offers a guarantee that the home will be a good security instrument for the money they are lending.

- ◆ If you buy new construction, take extra time to make certain you understand the financing. Temporary interest rate buy-downs with ultra-low payments are just that—temporary.

Chapter 12

Closing on the Loan

In This Chapter

- ◆ Escrow closings
- ◆ Round-table closings
- ◆ Your responsibility at the closing
- ◆ Understanding the HUD-1 Settlement Statement

The time has come to put you officially into debt. Up to now, there has not been any financial obligation between you and the lender. You could have at any time chosen to abandon the application, move to another company, or give up the idea entirely. You would have forfeited any money spent on your application fees and the time invested, but you hadn't committed yourself yet.

Now comes a meeting where documents will be signed and the transactions will be final. This meeting is referred to as the "closing." Two things happen at the closing: The seller transfers the deed and title to the property over to you, and the mortgagor transfers the money to the seller while placing a lien on your property.

The seller also turns over the property to you, based upon your contractual agreement. You can expect the keys, the garage door openers, and the manuals to the appliances.

But don't be alarmed if everything doesn't look perfect or go smoothly. Think about how many pieces need to come together at the same time and what needs to be reviewed, verified, and approved. The loan closing is notoriously known for rewrites and corrections. It's a time for patience but also for diligence because everyone wants it right before it's all sealed and delivered.

Round-Table Closing vs. Escrow Closing

The closing is the culmination of the purchase or the lending process. Although there are documents for both the buyer and the seller to sign, most of the paperwork is for the borrower. And depending upon which region of the country you're in and how your community is set up, you will have either a round-table closing or an escrow closing.

The round-table closing is the traditional method. Buyers and sellers have already decided as part of their purchase agreement the date of their settlement. And depending upon what may be customary in your marketplace, one of the parties will have been responsible for choosing the company that will facilitate the closing. Different parts of the country do it differently, but normally, the party that is responsible for paying the title insurance chooses the company.

It's Your Money

In the case of a refinance, the borrower chooses and often returns to the original settlement company because of discounts the company provides. Discounts include no survey, reduced closing fees, and credit on title insurance and the title search.

In the past, the traditional closing often took place in a bank office, with a representative of the bank facilitating the process. The buyers sat on one side of the table, the sellers on the other. If there was representation such as an attorney or a Realtor present, they took up seats next to their clients. Usually an abstract of the title was reviewed. Often as thick as a small book, the abstract showed all the ownership transfers and conveyances (transfer to title/ownership interest). The lender wanted to make certain that the buyer had free and clear ownership. The facilitator doled out the paperwork to be signed. At the end, everyone shook hands and exchanged keys and good wishes. The deal was done.

Today's process is much the same; however, instead of taking place at the bank's office, the transaction is done at an independent third-party site, usually a title insurance company, escrow agent, or attorney's office. In the early 1970s, banks chose to outsource the closing piece, for both efficiency and cost. This was also the time when mortgage money sources changed from primarily banks to the secondary market providers, Fannie Mae and Freddie Mac (see Chapter 7 for more information).

The description of closing could be portrayed in a Norman Rockwell print. But this closing is not without its own issues. If you're transacting with sellers, everyone needs to agree on a date and time. And lots of parties need to make the same time commitment. Settlement companies have relaxed their scheduling to accommodate closing at two different hours on the same day, if needed, but this is obviously duplication and thus not very cost-effective for them.

It can be more complicated when the seller is expecting his or her sales proceeds at closing and needs those funds to take to his or her loan closing on a new home. If there are delays or split times for signing, it may mean trips back and forth.

An escrow closing is done differently. The earnest money is held by an independent title insurance representative, escrow company, or attorney, who becomes the money "pass-through" resource. All cash from buyer, seller, and lender pass through this agency. And rather than set a specific date and time for closing, "the escrow" is open for a few days to allow for all disbursements to arrive. The information is then reconciled, and, at the end of the window, disbursements are made and the keys are delivered. Perhaps it's not as personal, but the closing is, after all, a business transaction and is handled as such.

The Flow of Information

Regardless of whether your closing is round-table or escrow, the movement of information and documentation is the same. Remember, the settlement agent is acting on behalf of the lender, as an intermediary for all parties. Think of this as the final act of a large production, where all parties come together for the grand finale. Usually there is a lot going on, and it's anything but flawless. The following flow chart gives you a visual overview of the entire process.

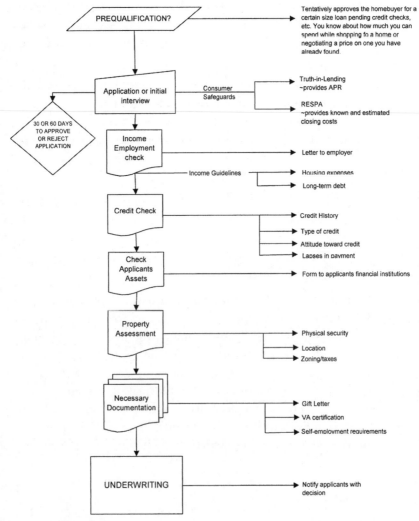

Mortgage flow chart.

The lender provides the closing company with instructions on how the loan paperwork should read, what fees need to be charged, and how the borrowers will be taking title. The lender also usually sends along the necessary documents to be signed. The Realtors and attorneys involved provide copies of the purchase agreement or contract that spells out the terms and conditions of the transaction.

In the meantime, the closing agent is compiling information on services performed and fees charged for such things as the survey, the pest inspection, and the county recorder's office, to name a few. Anyone who participates in any facet of the home purchase/home sale process that renders a service must be accounted for.

Then there is the research to make certain the property will be transferred correctly, with clear title. This means that someone will physically research county courthouse records to determine who may have placed a claim, lien, or encumbrance on the property in the recent past. Most of these services cannot be performed until after the mortgage is approved, which is usually only a couple of days before the loan is set to close.

So information comes to the settlement agent, and it is processed and reviewed and disbursed to the borrower, seller, and agents involved. And each of these participants must review and approve of those items they have brought to the table.

Usually, the settlement agent is providing the final dollar figure to the anxious borrower. And one of the most common complaints heard is how hard it is to get the final number. Is it any wonder, given the number of people and the task of accumulating all of the data needed?

A tip here is to get a worst-case scenario figure from the lender. The lender can usually provide you an accurate estimate, and if you pay too much, the settlement agent will refund you the difference. Have the check made payable to yourself so you can endorse it over once everything meets with your satisfaction.

It's always better to bring too much money than not enough. Most lenders cannot accept personal checks for any amount above $1,000.00.

The Documentation You'll Need to Have at Closing

If you don't pay cash for the home, then for a closing to take place, your lender will need to approve you for a loan and provide the settlement company with the appropriate paperwork to be signed. And in the approval, the lender will have specified what you need to complete the transaction with them. You should have been notified by letter of any outstanding conditions that must be satisfied to grant your loan. Normal conditions are, for example, verification that you've received your funds from an investment plan for closing. It's prudent to talk with the lender before arriving at the closing, to refresh yourself on what is still needed. There is a lot of activity surrounding the closing, and it's easy to forget or misunderstand what's needed.

> **Before You Sign** _____
>
> Rather than being pressured to read the fine print at the loan closing, request that the paperwork be available to read 24 to 48 hours prior to closing. Take it home the night before, read it, and make notes on questions you may have. The time at the closing then can be spent in summary rather than bewilderment. Under federal law, the borrower has a right to receive the HUD-1 Settlement Statement 24 hours prior to closing.

The settlement company will also require a few things from you. In most states, a photo ID is required to prove that you are who you sign you are. You will also be asked to provide evidence of homeowner's insurance, usually a policy and a paid receipt to show you actually purchased it. The insurance policy is required, regardless of whether you will be escrowing. The mortgage document specifies that you must have suitable insurance coverage at all times, and you must be able to provide proof at closing and upon request in the future.

The insurance provider will also ask you how the policy should be made out. The term most likely used is "mortgagee clause." Remember, you are in a partnership with the mortgage lender, and the policy will need to reflect the lender's name, address, and account number for reference. If there is a need to file a claim, both the borrower and the mortgagee will be covered.

It's Your Money

Because of fraud, most lenders no longer allow you to close escrow with a personal check. Expect to be asked to provide a cashier's check or to arrange for funds to be "wired" or electronically transferred to the settlement agent. If you intend to wire funds, prepare in advance. It can sometimes take a lead time of a few days to coordinate the transfer.

Be prepared to have your funds available in the form of a cashier's check or some form of currency recognized as cash. The good-funds law in most states requires that the money you put on the table at closing be immediately tendered. Your lender, your real estate agent, or the settlement company will tell you how much money you'll need. And if you've received good information from your lender, it will be close to what you've expected.

The average loan closing takes about one hour, and that's not much time to read through the forms that require your signature. You should schedule your closing so that the documents can be made available to you a couple days in advance. That way, you have time to read, make notes, and look for any corrections before you get to the big event.

It's Your Money

During the refinance of an owner-occupied residence, the lender must allow you three days after closing to change your mind, known as a rescission period. This practice was established to allow the borrower a cooling-off period and to make certain that they had not signed their paperwork under duress. The three-day right to rescind is not required on investment properties and second homes.

The HUD-1 Settlement Statement

It's hard to imagine how funds are dispersed if you've never been to a loan closing. There are expenses for the title company, the survey, the recorder's office, the home inspector, the termite company, the gas folks ... and the list grows.

OMB NO. 2502-0265

A.		B. TYPE OF LOAN	
U.S. DEPARTMENT OF HOUSING & URBAN DEVELOPMENT **SETTLEMENT STATEMENT**	1. ☐FHA 2.☐FmHA 3.☐CONV. UNINS. 4.☐VA 5.☐CONV. INS.		
	6. FILE NUMBER 05-EXAMPLE	7. LOAN NUMBER 23456	
	8. MORTGAGE INS CASE NUMBER		

C.   NOTE: This form is furnished to give you a statement of actual settlement costs. Amounts paid to and by the settlement agent are shown. Items marked "[POC]" were paid outside the closing; they are shown here for informational purposes and are not included in the totals.
1.0   3/98   (05-EXAMPLE.PFD/05-EXAMPLE/5)

D. NAME AND ADDRESS OF BORROWER	E. NAME AND ADDRESS OF SELLER	F. NAME AND ADDRESS OF LENDER
John Doe Jane Doe	Sam Seller Sara Seller	Mortgage Company USA 456 Money Street Borrowtown, Ohio 45678

G. PROPERTY LOCATION 123 Pleasantview Anywhere, OH 55556 Franklin County, Ohio	H. SETTLEMENT AGENT 31-1588128 The Title Link Agency, Ltd. PLACE OF SETTLEMENT 500 West Wilson Bridge Road, Ste 125 Worthington, OH 43085	I. SETTLEMENT DATE December 15, 2005

J. SUMMARY OF BORROWER'S TRANSACTION		K. SUMMARY OF SELLER'S TRANSACTION	
100. GROSS AMOUNT DUE FROM BORROWER:		**400. GROSS AMOUNT DUE TO SELLER:**	
101. Contract Sales Price	175,000.00	401. Contract Sales Price	175,000.00
102. Personal Property		402. Personal Property	
103. Settlement Charges to Borrower (Line 1400)	2,309.43	403.	
104.		404.	
105.		405.	
Adjustments For Items Paid By Seller in advance		*Adjustments For Items Paid By Seller in advance*	
106. City/Town Taxes to		406. City/Town Taxes to	
107. County Taxes to		407. County Taxes to	
108. Assessments to		408. Assessments to	
109.		409.	
110.		410.	
111.		411.	
112.		412.	
120. GROSS AMOUNT DUE FROM BORROWER	177,309.43	*420. GROSS AMOUNT DUE TO SELLER*	175,000.00
200. AMOUNTS PAID BY OR IN BEHALF OF BORROWER:		**500. REDUCTIONS IN AMOUNT DUE TO SELLER:**	
201. Deposit/earnest money $1,000.00 RETURNED		501. Excess Deposit (See Instructions)	
202. Principal Amount of New Loan(s)	166,250.00	502. Settlement Charges to Seller (Line 1400)	12,410.00
203. Existing loan(s) taken subject to		503. Existing loan(s) taken subject to	
204.		504. Payoff First Mortgage to Payoff Co.	102,367.78
205.		505. Payoff Second Mortgage	
206.		506.	
207.		507.	
208.		508.	
209.		509.	
Adjustments For Items Unpaid By Seller		*Adjustments For Items Unpaid By Seller*	
210. City/Town Taxes to		510. City/Town Taxes to	
211. County Taxes to		511. County Taxes to	
212. Assessments to		512. Assessments to	
213.		513.	
214.		514.	
215.		515.	
216.		516.	
217.		517.	
218.		518.	
219.		519.	
220. TOTAL PAID BY/FOR BORROWER	166,250.00	*520. TOTAL REDUCT. AMT DUE SELLER*	114,777.78
300. CASH AT SETTLEMENT FROM/TO BORROWER:		**600. CASH AT SETTLEMENT TO/FROM SELLER:**	
301. Gross Amount Due From Borrower (Line 120)	177,309.43	601. Gross Amount Due To Seller (Line 420)	175,000.00
302. Less Amount Paid By/For Borrower (Line 220)	(166,250.00)	602. Less Reductions Due Seller (Line 520)	(114,777.78)
303. CASH (X FROM) (TO) BORROWER	11,059.43	*603. CASH (X TO) (FROM) SELLER*	60,222.22

HUD-1 (3-86) RESPA, HB4305.2

The HUD-1 Settlement Statement—general information.

Page 2

L. SETTLEMENT CHARGES

	PAID FROM BORROWER'S FUNDS AT SETTLEMENT	PAID FROM SELLER'S FUNDS AT SETTLEMENT
700. TOTAL COMMISSION Based on Price $ 175,000.00 @ 6.0000 % 10,500.00		
Division of Commission (line 700) as Follows:		
701. $ 5,250.00 to Ace Real Estate		
702. $ 5,250.00 to Buy Real Estate		
703. Commission Paid at Settlement		10,500.00
704. to		
800. ITEMS PAYABLE IN CONNECTION WITH LOAN		
801. Loan Origination Fee % to		
802. Loan Discount % to		
803. Appraisal Fee to Mortgage Company USA POC $350.00		
804. Credit Report to Mortgage Company USA POC $35.00		
805. Tax Related Service Fee to Mortgage Company USA	75.00	
806. Processing Fee to Mortgage Company USA	150.00	
807. Underwriting Fee to Mortgage Company USA	100.00	
808. Flood Life of Loan Certificate to Mortgage Company USA	18.00	
809. Courier Fee to Mortgage Company USA	26.00	
810.		
811.		
900. ITEMS REQUIRED BY LENDER TO BE PAID IN ADVANCE		
901. Interest From 12/15/05 to 01/01/06 @ $ 27.328800/day (15 days 6.0000%)	409.93	
902. Mortgage Insurance Premium months		
903. Hazard Insurance Premium 1.0 years Insurance Co.	600.00	
904.		
905.		
1000. RESERVES DEPOSITED WITH LENDER		
1001. Hazard Insurance 2.000 months @ $ 50.00 per month	100.00	
1002. Mortgage Insurance months @ $ 96.97 per month		
1003. City/Town Taxes months @ $ per month		
1004. County Taxes 2.000 months @ $ per month		
1005. Assessments months @ $ per month		
1006. months @ $ per month		
1007. months @ $ per month		
1008. Aggregate Adjustment months @ $ per month		
1100. TITLE CHARGES		
1101. Settlement or Closing Fee to The Title Link Agency, Ltd.	185.00	35.00
1102. Abstract or Title Search to		
1103. Title Examination to The Title Link Agency, Ltd.		150.00
1104. Title Insurance Binder to The Title Link Agency, Ltd.	50.00	50.00
1105. Document Preparation to James Scott Stevenson, Attorney		35.00
1106. Notary Fees to		
1107. Attorney's Fees to		
(includes above item numbers:)		
1108. Title Insurance to The Title Link Agency, Ltd. as Agent for	100.00	975.00
(includes above item numbers:)		
1109. Lender's Coverage $ 166,250.00 100.00		
1110. Owner's Coverage $ 175,000.00 975.00		
1111. Courier/Express fee to The Title Link Agency, Ltd.	20.00	20.00
1112. Endorse EPA SURVEY to The Title Link Agency, Ltd.	125.00	
1113.		
1200. GOVERNMENT RECORDING AND TRANSFER CHARGES		
1201. Recording Fees: Deed $ 28.00; Mortgage $ 132.00; Releases $	160.00	
1202. City/County Tax/Stamps: Deed ; Mortgage	0.50	175.00
1203. State Tax/Stamps: Deed ; Mortgage		
1204.		
1205. Recordation Fee to The Title Link Agency, Ltd.	15.00	
1300. ADDITIONAL SETTLEMENT CHARGES		
1301. Survey to Surveying Co.	125.00	
1302. Pest Inspection to Termite Co.	50.00	
1303. Gas Warranty to Gas Co		75.00
1304. Home Warranty to Home Warranty Co.		395.00
1305.		
1400. TOTAL SETTLEMENT CHARGES (Enter on Lines 103, Section J and 502, Section K)	2,309.43	12,410.00

(05-EXAMPLE / 05-EXAMPLE / 5)

The HUD-1 Settlement Statement is a standard industry form that was designed to simplify the details. This document shows the expenses of the transaction. Both the borrower and the seller, if applicable, are represented on the same form.

Page 1 of the HUD-1 identifies the parties involved, the property address, the loan number, the lender name, and the loan type. It is meant to be the reference tool for the closing and summarizes the disbursement of the money. The form is split, and all applicable expenses are listed in the respective columns, identified, and totaled. Any credits, such as application fees or earnest money, are also listed so that, at the bottom, when all has been added and subtracted, the funds needed to settle are disclosed. This is where you get the magic number for funds needed for closing.

By the time you get to the closing, you should have a clear understanding of what money you'll need to have available. Let's look at the HUD-1 and correlate this form to the good faith estimate and truth-in-lending disclosures from the Uniform Residential Loan Application (see these in Chapters 4 and 7, respectively). You've learned that the forms should reflect approximately the same charges.

Let's begin our examination of the HUD-1 with page 2, where there is a series of 700 numbers at the top relating solely to the real estate commissions to be paid on the transaction. You'll see an entry for both the selling and listing agents and the amounts earned. Our example shows these fees charged to the seller. If in the atypical event you have hired your own representation and the seller does not acknowledge them, you could be responsible for the fee. Typically, the seller pays these fees.

The remainder of page 2 is similar to the good faith estimate document, itemizing the expenses for the transaction. This example has been completed to complement the previous transaction for clarity. Therefore, some of the fees noted here have no dollar attachment.

For example, Section 1000 for reserves refers to the escrow account. City taxes and any assessments required for settlement are noted here. Section 1100 title charges shows no fees for the abstract or title search because there was a title examination.

Section 1300 lists additional settlement charges, such as those paid for a pest inspection, home warranty program, or gas warranty. These warranties may be offered to you as part of the home purchase by the seller, or you may find that they are contractually required per the purchase contract. The gas warranty refers to gas line protection. A home warranty is a policy that covers the mechanics of a home, such as the heating and cooling system. If a repair is needed within a specified date of closing, this policy, if used, may offset some of the initial expense to the homebuyer. Again, there are regional differences in what additional settlement charges can be assessed; however, they all are located on page 2. Finally, line 1400 is the total of the columns to carry over to page 1.

The top third of page 1 is information on the loan type, loan number, and case number (if one has been assigned for either FHA or VA). The buyer, seller, and lender name and address are listed, along with the place of settlement and date. Most identification numbers are noted at the top of this form. The left side of the form is for the borrower, the right side for the seller.

Items 101/40l are the final agreed-upon price of the home.

Items 102/402 list any additional items to be sold with the home.

Item 103 is the closing costs from line 1400, page 2, for the borrower.

Items 106 through 112/406 through 412 are used if the taxes and any assessments are paid in advance of closing and there needs to be reconciliation.

Items 120/420 are the total of all expenses due by both parties to this point.

Item 201 reflects any earnest money deposits paid on the purchase contract. These monies are credited back to you, or you may see them returned.

Item 202 is the mortgage amount you have agreed upon.

Items 203/503 are used for a loan assumption.

Item 502 is the summary of expenses from line 1400 on page 2.

Item 504 is for the seller's existing loan payoff amount.

Item 505 applies if the seller has a second mortgage or home equity loan balance to be paid.

Items 210/510 are any monies set aside for city/town taxes.

Items 212/512 apply for any tax assessments.

Items 220/520 are column totals for the gross amount paid by and for the borrower, and due to the seller. The dollar amount on line Item 220 is the amount of money you have available from the lender and the seller to complete the transaction.

Items 301/601 are the gross amount from and to each party from line 120/420.

Items 302/602 reiterate the totals from 220/520.

Items 303/603 are final numbers from the borrower and final numbers due to the seller. Item 303 is the money you will need to have for closing after the loan amount has been subtracted.

By reviewing this format alongside your good faith estimate, you will begin to understand how the money moves. Once the settlement agent collects the money from the buyer, the agent is able to pay the seller the proceeds.

Rather than you writing 20 independent checks at closing, each item is summarized.

When your final dollar amount is confirmed by all parties, you must be prepared to have "good funds" available for the closing. Money needs to be available as cash and then put into a cashier's check to be presented at the closing. I've seen more than one closing delayed because good funds were not available. As you are moving around money or accumulating money for closing, it's important that it be in the institution that is going to issue you your final check no less than 10 days prior to the closing. Most banks require time to let the funds sit, to make certain that they are actually available. We've all deposited checks and had the bank say that there is a hold on the funds for several days. This is the same thing.

Lots of things must come together for the closing, so it's not unusual for corrections to be made on the day of your closing. Don't get caught up in the frenzy. You can always get your cashier's check for more than the exact amount. The closing agent is always happy to refund you the difference before you leave, and you'll find that it takes some of the stress out of the moment. Also, have the check made payable to yourself. Once you've signed your documents, you can endorse the check over to the closing company. If something goes wrong at the last minute, your funds are still in your possession.

> **It's Your Money**
>
> It's no coincidence that if you were to compare your lender good faith estimate with the closing statement, you would notice similarities in the format. A standard number-code system identifies fees and categorizes them according to who pays and what it is for. The truth-in-lending disclosure statement then uses specific sections in its calculation of the APR.

The title company gets instructions from the lender for the closing. The lender will provide a list of the fees it will be charging for the loan process. The settlement agent will also have expenses, for such things as the survey and the recording fees that will be added to the lender's expenses. The purchase contract will reveal any additional expenses per the agreement, such as the real estate fees. The title company completes the HUD-1.

Additional Documentation You'll Be Reviewing

The closing agent will usually have a stack of paperwork to review with you. And my experience has been that most of them do a fine job of introducing the document, highlighting its content, and showing where you need to sign and initial. We attempt here to introduce you to most of the documents, but each individual lender—and each state, for that matter—may have its own specific documents as well.

The note is the legal instrument that obligates you to repay the dollar amount you borrow to the lender.

The mortgage is the document that places a lien, or hold, on your real estate. The property, in effect, is the security to the lender that the note, or money, will be repaid.

A title examination is performed and the courthouse records are checked for present liens or claims against the property. The lender requires the examination as part of the closing process so that he or she can verify that when a lien is placed on the home, that lender is in *first position*, and no one else has a prior claim. The home is the lender's security, after all, if the debt is not repaid.

def•i•ni•tion

> **First position** means that the lender has a priority interest in the real property above all others, including the borrower (that is, the lender has a right to the property as an asset, per the terms of the mortgage or deed of trust). The lender's lien is to be paid off first. If another vendor or lender wants to stake a claim against the property, such as a second mortgage lender, the primary lender's lien should be satisfied before all others. The first position is of critical importance to the lender in case the borrower defaults on the loan obligation and the home is sold to satisfy that lien.

Two types of title insurance exist.

The *lender's policy* is issued as protection to the lender that the title examination is accurate and free from defects of title. In most states, the owner's policy is optional and would also protect the homeowner under the same terms. Your title insurance policy today serves the same purpose as your abstract of years past, but it is much thinner. An examiner goes to the courthouse and reviews public records for liens and transfers, but the entire history is not transferred.

The *title policy* provides coverage against any claims against the property before you take ownership. You are responsible going forward.

The *truth-in-lending disclosure statement* you received at application time now is prepared for the actual date of closing. You will have final information regarding the terms and the APR. It's a good practice to have your application information at hand to compare numbers so that all questions can be addressed at the closing.

There may be a *property survey* for your review and signature. The survey illustrates where the home you're buying or the one you presently live in is situated within the property boundaries. The survey will also show any easements and encroachments that you need to be aware of.

Most notably, utility easements that may run along the boundaries of your property are right-of-ways for the utility company. If you plant a flower bed on an easement and the utility company needs to dig up a line through the easement, there go your flowers. It's up to the title insurance company to determine whether anything on the survey could prohibit clear transfer of title. A garage built over a property line, for example, could be of concern.

The state, lender, settlement agent, or realty company may need to have a variety of disclosures signed. There may be a disclosure from the title company or lender that mentions the procedure for corrections that needs to be made on the documents, and how those errors will be handled. There is usually a first-payment-due letter, with information on where and when to send the payment, and the amount. You may also receive information about other services: direct deposit, automatic-payment withdrawal, and biweekly payment withdrawal.

The following is a list of a few disclosures you can expect to sign:

◆ **Name affidavit.** This verifies that the persons signing the documents are who they say they are. All aliases are also listed. For example, if James A. Doe were to be signing paperwork, they may also have Jimmy Doe, Jamie Doe, James Doe, and J. Doe listed on the affidavit to cover all bases.

◆ **Occupancy affidavit.** This verifies that you intend to occupy the property. This is the lender's way of confirming that you'll be in the home if they've approved the loan as owner-occupied.

◆ **Payment letter.** This disclosure gives you the breakdown of the monthly payment required, and when and where to send the payment.

◆ **4506.** This document is a government document that, once signed, authorizes the IRS to release to the requestor information on filed tax returns. The lender can request copies for up to 60 days from the date signed to determine whether what was received from the borrower was filed with the IRS.

Other forms may be standard to your market, so you may ask for specific forms when talking with or gathering information from the real estate board in your area.

Before You Sign _____

The lender may have you sign a form to allow him to review the tax returns filed with the IRS. To discourage fraud, the 4506 gives the lender the opportunity to audit information to verify that it matched what was provided at loan application. When you sign the form, be sure to limit the time the lender can go back to a maximum of 60 to 90 days from closing. Also note what items were provided, such as the 2002 tax return and 2001 and 2002 W-2s, to avoid unnecessary access to personal data.

Holding Title to a Property

In most states, you are given a couple of options on how you want to be shown as the owner of your property. There are regional differences in documents, but there are a couple of simple guides to consider. Common titles are the following:

- **Individual** refers to a single individual who is taking title alone. This could be described as an individual man or woman or an unmarried man or woman.

- **Joint** refers to ownership with another or others, commonly seen as a husband and wife, joint tenants, or tenants in common. Some states have other variations on vesting types.

- **Survivorship** refers to the automatic transfer of ownership in case one party dies. This is also seen as joint tenant with right of survivorship. This title avoids probate for the property.

The best way to determine which way to hold title is to talk with your attorney. Because of the complex estate-planning mandates, it's important to have the advice of a legal professional when choosing how you should hold title.

The general warranty deed is the official document used to show the transfer of ownership between seller and buyer. This is one form that only the seller signs at closing; once recorded, the borrower usually receives the original back for his or her records.

Tax Considerations of a Mortgage

Aside from having your own place, the next best part of owning a home is the tax benefit. Mortgage interest is deductible on home loans up to $1,000,000 and on second mortgages up to $100,000. So hold on to the settlement statement after closing; it will help you when you begin to prepare for your following year's tax filing.

To assist in your tax preparation, the lender will notify you of the amount of interest you sent during the previous year, so be on the look-out for form 1098, Mortgage Interest Deduction, from your mortgage holder in January. The lender sends the same data to the IRS. In addition to mortgage interest, any property taxes paid for the year on your behalf will be included on the notification.

In many cases, this is the first time a taxpayer has the opportunity to step up filing practices from the 1040EZ Form to the actual 1040 and the preparation of schedules. The schedules are an addendum to the main document that explain where the numbers on the 1040 come from. You use Schedule A to disclose home- and mortgage-related deductions. In some cases, even if you have a mortgage, the amount available to deduct is not enough to allow you to skip past what the government gives as the standard deduction. But for most people, the fact that you're a homeowner allows you to take into account other expenses.

It's Your Money

> Why overpay Uncle Sam if you can help it? The IRS has a great tool available to help you determine how much you want your employer to withhold from your paycheck each month for federal taxes. Go to their website at www.irs.gov/individuals and click on the calculator. Follow the directions and you'll find a good way to estimate the number of exemptions you should be taking.

Another tax-related item you will want to review after closing is how you are *withholding* income through your employer. When you were hired, you should have filled out as part of your hire packet a W-4 form. The W-4 tells your employer how much money you'd like to have subtracted from your income each month to cover the taxes you will owe

April 15 each year. Revisit that form. Because you now have an interest deduction, you may find that you can increase your *exemptions*, allowing a bit more money to flow to you monthly without worrying about having to pay Uncle Sam at the end of the year. It's like getting a raise without asking the boss.

A worksheet on the back of the form helps you figure out what number to place on the final line. You can also access an online calculator through the IRS website at www.irs.gov/individuals. Go through the form and fill out the details based on what you know to be true from your pay stub. When you get to the question of interest in the deductions section, pull the information from your mortgage statement or amortization schedule, and multiply by the appropriate number of months in the year. Pay attention to the month your mortgage payment started, and count months through the end of the year. Don't include the property taxes at this point—just the interest.

For example, suppose you purchased a home in May and sent your first mortgage payment to the lender in July. Your loan amount is $166,250 (the same as the amortization schedule in Chapter 8, so flip back to that document if you need to follow along). The interest portion of your payment was $928.92. Multiply that number by 6, the number of months you will pay for that year (July through December), and insert $5,573.52 for the amount of interest paid. Your monthly interest payments will only go down from this point, but this is still a conservative approach if you don't include the property taxes. The calculator will then guide you to determine how many exemptions you can claim. This is only the first year's calculation and only a partial year of interest, so you may need to repeat this process in subsequent years.

You can also ask for the assistance of a tax professional who knows your finances, or wait until you've cycled through the first year to see what happens. In a nutshell, if you're getting a refund, your tax preparer may tell you that the exemption needs to go up so that less tax is withheld.

If you've paid discount points or an origination fee, you may also be able to write off those expenses. As long as they have been paid and have not been financed as part of the loan, they are considered interest and fall as a deduction in the year paid. The exception to this is that if, in a refinance, the points are financed into the loan, the deduction is carried through the remaining loan term.

Property taxes can also be taken as a deduction on your tax return. Some parts of the country handle the payment of taxes differently. In the Midwest, for example, taxes are frequently assessed and paid in arrears. This means that at the end of the year, the property tax benefit for the home may belong to the seller, not the buyer.

The advice of tax professionals can often be more valuable than their fee when it comes to how to best utilize a home purchase for tax purposes.

def•i•ni•tion

Arrears is the result of a payment that is rendered after the due date rather than in advance of the due date.

The Least You Need to Know

♦ Information needed for a loan closing is compiled by the closing agent from many sources and may take time to accumulate.

♦ There are different closing methods: Round-table closing allows for all parties to meet to sign, and escrow closing charges a separate company with the task of reconciling and distributing funds within a window of time.

♦ Ask for closing documents, including the HUD-1 settlement statement, 24 to 48 hours prior to closing, to allow yourself time to formulate questions.

♦ There are many documents to sign at closing, several of which may have regional specific requirements. It is always best to check with a local representative for up-to-date disclosure requirements.

Chapter 13

Refinancing Your Home

In This Chapter

- ◆ Deciding whether to refinance
- ◆ Choosing the right refinancing option
- ◆ Finding a good refinancing deal
- ◆ Using home equity loans

Falling interest rates typically pique the consumer's awareness of the refinancing process. When rates are drifting downward, it's only normal to want to take advantage of the lower rates and the savings they bring because, as you know, lower is better. But how is it better? Obviously, if the interest rate is lower, the payment should also be lower. But are there other benefits worth considering when presented with the opportunity to rewrite the mortgage loan? These questions and more are answered in this chapter.

What Is a Refinance?

A loan that is rewritten on the same property but under different terms is called a refinance. When a borrower refinances, he or she is, in effect, paying off one mortgage and replacing it with another. The new loan can be done with the same lending institution or with someone else. Regardless, the loan is treated as if it were new, so there are always costs to be paid. Some services may be carried over from one mortgage to another, but count on the fees being similar to those of a purchase.

What Can Refinancing Help You Do?

The promise of lower house payments leads most borrowers to seek out the most attractive rates advertised. But you've learned that it's imperative to review the closing costs and interest rates side by side. Be leery of the offers that lure you to consider refinancing "with no money out of your pocket." The age-old saying about looking too good to be true applies well here.

There are many reasons to consider a refinance. The first is to lower your monthly payment. When you're following your budget and a payment goes down, it's a bonus. Money either can be redirected to another bill or perhaps can go into a savings plan. Ask the question, "What would I do with that extra cash monthly?" Think about what that money really means to you. Remember, most people think they are refinancing to save money.

So let's assume that the extra money would come in very handy to pay extra toward another monthly obligation. That's good because, in essence, you're using those dollars to improve your overall debt ratio. What if you don't have a plan in place for the extra money? Chances are, you'll find that the savings disappear, never to be realized anywhere.

Now, let's assume that the house payment is comfortable, but, like millions of others, you need to take advantage because lower is better. What about refinancing to keep the payment about the same, but perhaps lower the term, or the number of years, you're obligated to pay? Consider going from a 30-year loan to a 20-year loan. Each month you make your payment going forward, a larger portion is being applied to principal. The savings would not be in your pocket exactly, but it's sitting in the equity of your home. It's a plan; you've thought through why you're refinancing, and have used the rate to benefit you in another way.

Perhaps your mortgage can help with debt management. If you have equity built up, you may be able to tap that savings account to reduce or eliminate other obligations. Or that nest egg could be available for a home-improvement project, the down payment for a second home at your favorite vacation spot, or even college tuition. Mortgages are a desirable way to finance liabilities because of their inherent tax benefit, the interest write-off.

When Is the Best Time to Refinance?

Over the last four years, this question has been one of the most common heard by mortgage lenders around the country. And there is not a quick answer. People used to think that unless you could save 2 percent in the interest rate, it was not a good idea to refinance, but that thinking has changed. Instead of getting caught up in the rate game, evaluate your financial circumstances. You may find that the rate will help your decision along, but the cash flow and your long-term goals should really guide you in the decision.

When you originally settled on a loan program, you evaluated what your comfort level was. Through that process, you may not have surmised as much, but you made some decisions on long-term objectives. For example, if you chose a 7/1 ARM loan over a 30-year fixed, most likely you weighed the risks of the adjustments at the end of the eighty-fourth month against the value of the interest rate on the fixed-rate loan. In other words, you decided that either you did not intend to stay in the home longer than seven years, or the rate difference between the 7-year loan and the 30-year loan didn't matter enough to sway you to the conservative side. The lower monthly payment may have also been a deciding factor. Either way, you needed to think through what the home loan was going to accomplish for you long term.

As you contemplate a refinance, the same process occurs again. But this time, you're asking a few other questions. Where are you at this point in your life financially? Is your debt balanced with your savings, or are you too heavy in debt? Is your savings portfolio diverse? Do you have a fair distribution of assets—for example, money market, CD, real estate?

Realize that you're a homeowner now, and with that comes the responsibility of real estate investment. Regardless of whether you have 1 unit (your home) or 100 units, the value of that asset plays into your investment portfolio.

If you can see the opportunity to either save money monthly or better your cash-flow position and recover your expenses within a reasonable amount of time (it's good to break even at 12 to 18 months; refer to the "Discount Points and the Permanent-Rate Buy-Down" section in Chapter 10), then it's a good time. If you're fulfilling a long-term goal, such as withdrawing equity to reinvest in another asset, then it's okay to refinance.

Otherwise, rethink the refinance.

The Cost to Refinance

When you refinance a property, you are taking out a new loan. And when a new loan is established, expect to pay closing costs again. But it stands to reason that because you already have a loan, some of the expenses should be unnecessary or, at the least, offered at a discount.

For example, the lender will typically want a re-evaluation of the home, but rather than a full loan appraisal, you may find that they may only drive by the property and make a visual observation to determine that it is in place and verify its basic condition. Or the lender may rely on market statistics to verify that the property is in an area where values are increasing rather than decreasing. Both of these reviews are considerably less expensive than a full mortgage loan appraisal. You can expect to save $100 to $200 on a reduced review.

As for the closing fees, if you have your title policy from the previous loan closing, the title agency or escrow company will typically research the history of the property only from the date of the last loan closing through the present, as long as 10 years have not elapsed. By reducing the time to search public records, the cost is reduced and should save you approximately $100 in expenses.

If you can provide your property survey and can state that no structures have been built near or on the property lines, usually another survey can be avoided. A survey usually costs $125 to $175.

The closing company should offer to perform the closing at a reduced cost, as a professional courtesy, particularly for a repeat customer. Expect to save $50 to $100 from the original closing.

But some expenses cannot be avoided, such as recording fees, conveyance taxes, and document-preparation fees. And it's particularly important to understand the cost of the refinance in relation to the benefit of the savings. By minimizing the up-front costs of rewriting the loan, you are more likely to regain your investment within a reasonable time. Be aware of paying for discount points and excess fees, regardless of whether they're paid at closing or are rolled into the loan. The exercise in the section "Determining How Much Your Refinance Saves You," later in this chapter, illustrates this concept.

Documentation Needed to Refinance

As with the closing costs and the duplication of information, your lender may be able to get away with abbreviated paperwork for the refinance. For example, both FHA and VA loan programs allow for a "streamline" refinance that often can avoid the need for an appraisal, income, or asset information. The idea is this: if the overall payment is lower, or less than 20 percent greater than the existing payment, why go back and verify whether the borrower can afford the loan?

A credit report is requested to make certain that the loan is current, but otherwise, no new qualification analysis is done. This is a great way to take advantage of lower rates, without the scrutiny of a requalification.

And to save on closing costs (as mentioned earlier), you will be asked to provide the title policy and property survey from your previous loan closing. It is also helpful if you can give the lender information on your homeowner's insurance policy because the new loan will need to reflect that information.

> **It's Your Money**
>
> A common VA refinance is the IRRRL (interest rate reduction refinance loan). It requires no appraisal and no verification of income or assets. FHA also offers a streamlined refinance, and depending upon the loan circumstances, this may or may not require an appraisal and credit qualifying.

Types of Refinances

Refinances are categorized by what purpose the new loan will serve. A *rate/term* refinance denotes that the interest rate or the number of years remaining on the loan will change. In most cases, the borrower is either improving his or her cash flow or trying to build equity faster. Closing costs may be included as part of the balance of the mortgage. This is known as "wrapping fees into the loan" in some parts of the country.

Before You Sign

Should you take your equity out of the home through a refinance or a home equity loan/line of credit? A couple considerations are these: one payment versus two, payment comparison, risk of payment increase in a line of credit, LTV restrictions, and prepayment of loan versus amortization over term.

If any additional expenses are added into the loan amount, such as cash-to-payoff debt, the refinance is considered an *equity take-out*. Regardless of the type of refinance, the lender will want you to keep some of the equity in the home, usually 10 to 25 percent. There are exceptions to these guides, but remember that when you deviate from the norm, risk and rate typically go up. The property value will be determined through a reappraisal of the home.

The new loan may also require new verifications of income, assets, and credit. But many lenders offer a streamlined refinance, which may eliminate or significantly reduce additional documentation and qualification. This option may be available if you are changing the rate or term and the payment does not increase dramatically (no greater than 20 percent). No cash may be taken through the loan other than for closing costs.

What's Different About a Refinance Loan?

The basic process of obtaining the mortgage loan will not change. You'll need to decide what the loan is for and how you would like it structured. The lender will provide payment and cost information that you'll need to compare to evaluate which option suits your long-range goals.

The closing cost considerations are different. When you purchased, the costs were paid up front, either by you or by the seller. When you refinance, you have a choice of paying the expenses or financing them into the loan. The common way to handle closing costs as part of the loan is to increase the loan balance. Another solution is for the lender to cover the expenses as part of the rate. The par rate is no extra money out of pocket, as discussed in Chapter 10. If that rate goes down, the cost of the money goes up, hence discount points. But as the rate goes up, money is paid back to the borrower and is available to cover closing costs. So when you see lenders advertising no money out of pocket, they're using either the rate or the loan to cover the costs to refinance.

It is a cost to you if the rate goes up because the lender is covering your costs. It is a cost to you if the mortgage balance is increased to cover your refinance. Even if you don't write a check for the costs, they're in the loan somewhere. So lenders who say "no money out of pocket" may be bending the truth.

You'll need to think through whether you want to finance the costs or pay them up front as part of closing. When you refinance, it's as though you've taken a new loan. You'll skip a house payment, leaving you a free month to either cover a portion, if not all, of your refinance expenses or walk away with the equivalent of your house payment for that month.

If you finance your costs to refinance, you're taking from the house savings, and if you're trying to save money, you've spent money before saving it. By paying for the cost up front, your cash flow remains constant, and you've not used the equity to finance your cost of doing business. An exception is when you're reducing the term of the loan, such as when going from a 30-year to a 20- or 15-year term. If you finance your costs, it's not quite so bad because each payment made going forward has a significantly higher principal portion, and you're able to recover the cost of doing the refinance through the additional equity payments.

Determining How Much Your Refinance Saves You

How can you tell if you're saving money with a refinance? A couple of key calculations help you to compare today's loan to a new mortgage. Here is an example, with a table that follows for you to fill in yourself.

Refinance for Rate Reduction

Today's P&I payment	$1,000.00
New P&I payment	–850.00
Total savings	=150.00
Cost to refinance	2,500.00
Months to recover expense ($2,500.00 ÷ $150.00)	=16.67

Refinance for Cash Out

Today's P&I payment	$1,000.00
Other debts to be paid off	+525.00
Total expenses	=1,525.00
New P&I payment	–850.00
Savings monthly	675.00
Cost to refinance	2,500.00
Months to recover expense ($2,500.00 ÷ $675.00)	=3.7

Refinance for Rate Reduction

Today's P&I payment	_____
New P&I payment	–_____
Total savings	=_____
Cost to refinance	_____
Months to recover expense (_____ ÷ _____)	=_____

Refinance for Cash Out

Today's P&I payment	_____
Other debts to be paid off	+_____
Total expenses	=_____

Refinance for Cash Out

New P&I payment	–_____
Savings monthly	_____
Cost to refinance	_____
Months to recover expense (_____ ÷ _____)	=_____

The idea on any refinance is to know why you are refinancing and how the monthly savings will be applied. In the case of a rate/term refinance, the overall interest paid should be reduced, saving you money over the life of the loan. If you choose to do a cash-out refinance to consolidate debt, you will probably see your overall cash flow improve, saving you money.

Again, "savings" means different things to different households. You want to refinance only if you can foresee the benefit and recover the expense to do so within 12 to 18 months. Any longer time leaves open the question of whether the money spent to refinance will be recovered.

The Home Equity Loan vs. Refinancing

A refinance will cost you money to do, and sometimes that may defeat your purpose. If you're looking for quick, inexpensive cash out of your home, you might explore a home equity loan or line of credit. The lender will typically do an abbreviated credit/income check and a drive-by appraisal of your home. The lender then will offer you a loan based upon a percentage of your home value. That maximum loan amount available may vary from lender to lender. You may have more cash available to you by using a home equity product versus refinancing because the guides are different.

The rate is based upon the amount of the credit line, your credit score, and how much equity would be remaining in the home if the credit line were run up to its maximum. There are rarely significant closing costs to obtain the equity loan, which makes them attractive. Because home equity loans are easy to obtain, everybody seems to think they need one. Be cautious. As with any available credit, this is for emergencies and is not meant to be abused.

> **It's Your Money**
>
> A whole separate process exists for refinance loans in New York. Called extension, consolidation, and modification agreements, this is their form of a refinance. Rather than the traditional references we've made here, you will need to find guides specific to New York.

The disadvantage to the second mortgage is that there is another payment to contend with, and depending on whether it's fixed or an interest-only revolving loan, the payment movement could be a consideration. It's prudent to compare whether one solution is better than the other.

Reverse Mortgage

Another way to access the equity in your home is through an innovative loan solution known as a reverse mortgage. In a traditional mortgage, you pay the lender; in a reverse mortgage, the lender actually pays you a set amount of money. This loan solution was created to alleviate the need for retired homeowners to sell or refinance their home to access money to live on or to use for home improvements.

To be eligible, you must be at least 62 years old and live in the property. There are no income restrictions, and you can use the money as needed. There may be a limit to the amount you can draw each month, based upon your age and the value of the home. You can opt for monthly payments or set up a loan similar to a home equity line of credit that is available upon demand. The homeowner retains the title and continues to maintain the property, and is responsible for the taxes and insurance.

The loan does not normally need to be paid back while you live in the home. When the home is sold, the lien holder will realize the net proceeds after the sale to pay off the loan.

Loan Modification

In rare instances, the lender may allow you to rewrite the loan without refinancing. A loan modification keeps the original terms the same; for example, if it's a 30-year loan at 6.5 percent, the loan will stay as such. But if you have a significant payment toward principal, the lender may be willing to "modify" your payment based upon the new outstanding balance. This process could enable you to take advantage of a lower payment without the expense of refinancing the loan.

Tax Considerations with Refinances

In general, you are permitted to deduct interest paid and property taxes paid in the year they are paid. When it comes to refinancing, you are often given the option to finance closing costs and prepaid expenses for taxes and insurance, as value permits. If you elect to do so, you are effectively amortizing the expense of the fees to refinance over the loan's life. In doing so, you may be impacting how much of these expenses can be written off for tax purposes.

And because you are rearranging your payment, expect that the interest you pay yearly will adjust. Having said that, you can also expect that your deductible interest will be modified. It's a good idea to evaluate how this modification will affect you on tax day. Always consult with a tax professional to evaluate the impact.

Conclusion

The purpose of any guide book is to inform ... because information is power. And there is no other way to go but informed when financing a home. Too much of your hard-earned savings is on the line to proceed any other way. After all, your home is not merely the place you lay your head at night. As you've learned, it is an integral part of your financial makeup. And depending upon your long-term goals, this purchase may be a long-term asset or one that will be traded within a few years for another.

And by preparing yourself and understanding the options available, you can assure yourself that the decisions you make will be sound. Align yourself with experts. A lender can provide good information that you can understand. An informed real estate professional can provide more insight and information than you can compile, assuming that he or she is educated in the market you want to purchase in. An attorney can offer guidance as well as referrals to professionals within the industry. And a knowledgeable tax advisor can answer all your questions regarding how this purchase affects you going forward.

Keep in mind when you start the mortgage loan process that it is exactly that—a process. There is a starting point and a yet undetermined end. In the middle is the research and exploration. You've taken a very important step toward the end by reading this book.

The Least You Need to Know

- When refinancing, make certain you understand why and how you are benefiting from the process.

- Refinancing means you are rewriting the note, and with that process comes additional fees, some of which were paid previously when you purchased the home. There may be some credits available.

- There are two major types of refinance: rate/term and cash-out.

- Today there are other ways to obtain the equity or savings from your home. Aside from refinancing, you may consider opening a second mortgage to access the money in your home.

Glossary

abstract   A summary of land records pertaining to a parcel of land for public record.

acceleration   (1) The lender's right to ask for payment in full once a loan is in default. (2) To increase, as in the advance payment of principal on a loan.

adjustable-rate mortgage (ARM)   A loan program with a rate that will change periodically to reflect current market rates using a preset monetary indicator, known as an index. (*Also see* index, margin).

adjustment period   Refers to when and how often a rate can change on an adjustable-rate mortgage.

agent   One who represents you in a business or legal transaction.

amortization   Repayment of a liability with a portion of the payment being applied toward the principal balance as well as the interest owed.

amortization schedule   A summary through the life of a loan that shows the payment distribution toward principal and interest as each payment is made.

annual   Reflects activity for a year.

annual percentage rate (APR)   A federal required calculation that shows the cost of the mortgage yearly, based upon fees paid to obtain the loan. The APR is usually higher than the actual interest rate and is used by borrowers to compare lenders' fees.

annuity   An investment that is tied to an insurance policy that pays a rate of return.

appraisal   An opinion of value based upon factual analysis.

appraisal report   The written report done to support the value that lists the supporting data used to render the opinion; supporting data may include property that has sold recently within a specified market area.

appraised value   The final dollar amount the appraisal data supports.

appraiser   Licensed property examiner, authorized to render opinion of value.

appreciation   The additional value accrued on an investment, even due to inflation.

arm's-length transaction   A transaction in which there is no relationship between the parties that would interfere with the legitimacy of the exchange.

arrears   The result of a payment that is rendered after the due date rather than in advance of the due date.

assessment   Valuation; also an expense levied by a local municipality or association for a property-related service, such as a maintenance item or upgrade installation.

assets   Everything that is owned and tangible with a cash value.

assignment   To transfer the rights and warranty of a property to another entity.

assumption   An agreement that allows a seller to transfer title and terms of an obligation to the borrower, which can save the borrower closing expenses. Usually this transaction requires lender approval to legally transfer the liability of the debt.

attorney   A legal professional.

automated underwriting system (AUS)   An underwriting program that evaluates the creditworthiness of an applicant based on statistical data.

automated valuation model (AVM)   Appraisal software that evaluates the value of a home based on data gathered from public records on other homes that have sold in the area.

balloon loan   A short-term fixed-rate loan that is scheduled to be paid in full prior to the end of its amortization, leaving a balance to be paid; preset when the loan was established.

balloon payment   The last payment due on a balloon loan that satisfies the balance due.

bankruptcy   Federal statute that allows a debtor to be discharged of insurmountable financial obligations, with property and assets of the debtor being relinquished to the creditors in return.

binder   A report issued to state the terms of the policy that will be issued if all terms and conditions are met.

biweekly mortgage   Accelerated repayment of a mortgage obligation, with half of a monthly payment paid every two weeks. This allows for 26 payments versus 12 if paid monthly, and additional prepayment of principal as a result.

blanket mortgage   A mortgage that uses more than one property to secure the loan.

blended rate   The comparison of two loans, perhaps a first and second mortgage obligation, showing the effective rate when calculated together.

blue book value   The value of property as a capital asset, minus depreciation.

bond   (1) An asset, such as a government-issued savings bond. (2) A form of financing long-term debt issued by a government municipality that pays a return to the investor.

borrower   One who applies for and receives a loan, with the intention of repaying the obligation.

bridge loan/bridge financing   A short-term note to take equity from a present home for down payment and fees for closing on a new home, rather than waiting for proceeds from sale.

broker   One who arranges the financing or negotiates a sale for a fee.

bundling   Putting together several services under one entity. An example of bundling is when a lender or real estate company takes care of an appraisal, title examination, and home inspection.

buy-down   A subsidy that reduces the monthly payment for a period of time, either full time or temporary. *See* permanent interest rate buy-down.

caps (interest)   The maximum rate increase allowable per the loan, as a protection to the borrower.

caps (payment)   The maximum payment increase allowable per the loan, as a protection to the borrower.

cash flow   The amount of cash received from income-producing property to cover the payment, maintenance, and expenses.

cash out   Refinance that draws equity or money out of the present home.

cash reserves   Money remaining and accessible to you when you have completed the transaction.

cashier's check   A bank-issued check that is acceptable in lieu of cash, drawn against actual funds available.

caveat emptor   "Let the buyer beware." The buyer should review the property and be satisfied with its condition before accepting ownership. Legislation is in place stating that the seller has no responsibility to disclose known defects, but the seller cannot hide them or lie if asked.

ceiling   The maximum amount an interest rate can adjust.

certificate of deposit (CD)   A savings method with a preset rate of return and duration, usually without opportunities to withdraw.

certificate of eligibility (COE)   A document that entitles the holder to a VA loan if he or she meets several requirements, issued by the VA after review of the application (Form 1880 and a copy of the DD214, or a statement of service, if still enlisted).

certificate of reasonable value (CRV)   The report issued by the Veteran's Administration to establish current market value.

certificate of veteran status   Document provided by the VA that entitles those eligible to abbreviated financing benefits for lower down payments on an FHA mortgage loan.

chattel   Personal property included, but unrelated to the sale of the home.

child-care statement   Letter required from a child-care provider evidencing the cost of child care.

clear title   Unchallenged ownership of a property.

closing   The meeting or process by which mortgage papers are executed or the transfer of ownership between buyer and seller occurs (also known as settlement).

closing costs   Fees associated with transferring real estate ownership or obtaining a mortgage loan.

closing statement   The document that reconciles the settlement fees for both borrowers and sellers at closing.

co-borrower/co-mortgagor   One who becomes obligated for the repayment of a loan with the primary loan maker; both have equal liability for repayment. Also called *co-signer.*

co-ownership   Ownership by two or more parties.

co-signer/co-maker   One who becomes obligated for the repayment of a loan with the primary loan maker; both have equal liability for repayment. Also called *co-borrower.*

collateral   Property used to secure or guarantee a loan.

commercial bank   A banking institution that offers checking, savings, installment, and construction loans and other services not offered by the savings and loan associations.

commitment   A written promise to make, insure, or purchase a loan that notes any stipulations; a rate-lock guarantee.

commitment fee   Fee collected by a lender to lock in or guarantee an interest rate.

commitment letter   Document that outlines lender or investor promises and stipulations.

common area   The area within a multifamily property or neighborhood that is accessible to all.

Community Reinvestment Act   Federal legislation passed in 1977 to encourage banks and thrifts to open lending practices within the institution's immediate neighborhood or community.

comparables   Similar properties used to establish value for a property appraisal.

competitive market analysis (CMA)   A method of establishing value by comparing sales prices of comparable homes recently sold.

condominium   A development of two or more units, with owners owning individual space within the walls of the unit but having joint ownership in common areas.

conforming loan   A mortgage loan that meets the requirements of the secondary market lending the money, by either qualification guidelines or maximum loan amount.

conforming loan limit   Maximum loan amounts set by the secondary market for its loan programs.

consent form   Authorization for the lender to compile applicable data for a home loan.

construction loan   A short-term loan that takes a newly built home from the ground up through completion of the home, usually substituted with a mortgage loan to pay off at the end.

consumer lending   Loans for household appliances and personal property such as automobiles.

contingency   Consent based upon a stipulation, such as a new-home purchase contingent upon the sale of the present residence.

contract of sale   Written agreement to purchase, which lists all terms and conditions of the sale.

conventional loan   A mortgage loan other than a government-insured FHA/VA loan.

convertible mortgage   An adjustable-rate loan that can be turned into a fixed-rate loan as described in the terms and conditions of the mortgage note. Not all ARM loans can be converted to a fixed-rate loan.

conveyance   Transfer of title or ownership interest.

cooperative (co-op)   A property type in which the residents own a share of the corporation that holds the property as an asset.

correspondent lender   Lenders that use their own resources to close a loan but transfer it immediately after closing to another mortgage banker to service.

cost approach   Property-appraisal practice of calculating the replacement cost of the dwelling plus land value, minus depreciation.

cost of funds index (COFI)   An adjustable-rate mortgage indicator that uses the San Francisco area as an indicator. Also known as the 11th District Cost of Funds index.

counteroffer   A response to an offer made, often seen in real estate transactions.

covenant   Agreement that spells out assurances and rights.

credit   History in regard to establishing and paying liabilities.

credit limit   The maximum amount of credit that has been extended.

credit report   A written summary of credit history, which reflects repayment practices and amount of indebtedness.

credit score   A statistical evaluation of a borrower's creditworthiness based upon credit usage, type of available credit, and repayment schedules. Scores range from 350 to 900, with 900 being superior.

creditor   One to whom you owe a liability.

debt   A liability that you owe.

debt service   The total amount of installment and revolving credit owed.

debt-to-income ratio   Gross monthly income is divided into the proposed housing expense, which includes the taxes and insurance as a first calculation; income is divided into the proposed housing expense plus monthly revolving/installment debt for a second calculation.

deed   A conveyance or financing instrument for transferring ownership.

deed in lieu (of foreclosure)   A deed transferring ownership to the lender to avoid foreclosure proceedings.

deed of trust   A document used in place of a mortgage in many states, securing the payment of the note to the lender.

default   Failure to meet or pay on monthly obligations in a timely fashion.

deferred interest   An agreement in which the lender accepts less than the actual payment, and the uncollected portion is added back to the loan balance.

deficiency judgment   The amount the borrower is liable for if the sheriff's sale does not bring enough proceeds to cover the outstanding indebtedness.

deflation   Decrease in the source of money or credit.

delinquency   Failure to make on-time payments.

demand note   A note that has no specified date of repayment, due at the lender's discretion.

Department of Veteran's Affairs (formerly the Veterans' Administration)   A government agency in place to ensure the rights and benefits to veterans and their survivors, one of which includes the entitlement of a no- or low-down-payment home loan.

depreciation   The loss of value for an asset due to condition or extended use.

direct endorsement   Federal Housing Administration loan feature authorizing lenders to act on its behalf when rendering decisions regarding FHA-insured home loans.

discharge   To be released from obligation or service.

discount point   The cost associated with purchasing a lower-interest rate than the prevailing market; considered prepaid interest.

discrimination   Refusal or unfair decision-making process based upon the party's race, sex, or nationality.

document stamp   A closing expense in some states that shows the amount of tax paid for the transfer of the property.

down payment   Difference between the sales price and the amount borrowed, paid either out of savings or with funds from outside sources.

due on sale   A clause that allows the lender to receive 100 percent repayment of the loan when the property transfers ownership.

earnest money   Good-faith money deposited with a third party to reinforce the borrower's intention to purchase.

easement   A right to use someone else's land for a specific purpose, such as placement of utilities.

economic obsolescence   Depreciation of property value due to its physical location rather than its actual condition.

effective income   Verifiable, reliable income that's assumed to be ongoing after expenses.

eminent domain   The right of the government to take and purchase private property at a fair market value for public use.

employment verification   Letter or verbal confirmation of job status, income, and likelihood of continuance.

encroachment   An extension of a wall, fence, or building from one's property onto the neighbors' property.

encumbrance   A financial or physical security claim on a property that must be satisfied before a property can be conveyed.

entitlement   The VA loan benefit that allows eligibility for the housing benefit.

Equal Credit Opportunity Act (ECOA)   The federal law that requires lenders to offer loans equally regardless of race, color, religion, national origin, age, sex, marital status, or receipt of income from public assistance.

equity   The difference in the market value versus the indebtedness of an asset, also known as owner's interest or savings.

equity loan   A loan against the equity in a home. *See* home equity line of credit and home equity loan.

escrow   Deed transfers and earnest deposits held by a third party pending satisfaction of contingency for closing.

escrow account   An account held by the lender into which the borrower deposits monthly payments for property taxes, homeowner's insurance, and private insurance, if applicable. The lender makes these payments from the account.

execute   To complete or fulfill.

Fair and Accurate Credit Transmission Act (FACTA)   New legislation added to the Fair Credit Reporting Act specifying how information should be shared to protect the privacy of the individual.

Fair Credit Reporting Act (FCRA)   Legislation that provides borrowers a free copy of their report if they are denied credit, with assistance to correct invalid information.

Fannie Mae   *See* Federal National Mortgage Association.

Farmers Home Loan (FmHA)   A lending arm available on rural property, so named because the loans are often used by farmers.

Federal Deposit Insurance Corporation (FDIC)   Federal department for banking that insures depositors up to $100,000 in loss.

Federal Home Loan Bank Board (FHLBB)   The former regulatory agency for thrifts and savings and loans, now called the Office of Thrift Supervision.

Federal Home Loan Mortgage Corporation (FHLMC)   Known as Freddie Mac, a semigovernmental agency that provides mortgage financing through the secondary market for conventional as well as FHA mortgages.

Federal Housing Administration (FHA)   Department within the Division of Housing and Urban Development (HUD) that insures and regulates government housing made by private lenders for FHA mortgages.

Federal National Mortgage Association (FNMA)   Known as Fannie Mae, a private corporation created by Congress that provides money for one out of seven conventional residential mortgages provided nationally.

Federal Reserve Board   The governing body that sets monetary policy for banks.

Federal Savings and Loan Insurance Corporation (FSLIC)   A federal organization that insures deposits in savings and loans up to $100,000.

fee appraiser   Independent appraiser who does not work for the company he or she appraises for.

fee simple   The owners of the property have the right to dispose of the property as they wish, either by will or inherited.

FHA Amendatory Clause   Disclosure signed by all parties stating that the borrower is not held liable to complete the purchase transaction unless the value of the home is determined to be at a minimum equivalent to the sales price.

FHA mortgage insurance premium (MIP)   Insurance paid by the borrower on behalf of the lender to assure the lender if loan defaults, the federal government will reimburse the borrower's indebtedness.

FICO   A reference to a credit score named after Fair, Isaac and Company, which developed the system of scoring.

first mortgage   A lien on real property with the first right of satisfaction, taking priority over all others.

fixed-rate mortgage (FRM)   A loan in which the interest rate is the same throughout the loan's duration.

float   The option to take a wait-and-see approach rather than to lock in or guarantee an interest rate.

float down   A locked loan feature that allows the borrower to receive a lower interest rate if rates drop after the loan is locked.

flood insurance   Insurance to protect the dwelling against loss due to flooding, usually required for homes located in a floodplain. It may not cover personal belongings.

foreclosure   The legal right of the lender to force a sale of the asset (home) when the terms of the note have not been met to recover the lender's expenses.

Freddie Mac   *See* Federal Home Loan Mortgage Corporation.

free and clear   Ownership without any liens or encumbrances.

fully indexed rate The total of the index plus margin on an adjustable-rate mortgage.

funding The transfer of money from the lender to the borrower and/or their closing agent to complete the loan process.

gift A solicited or unsolicited transfer of asset, without recourse.

gift letter Confirmation of the transfer of a gift showing the amount and the giftor, and stating that there is no required repayment or obligation.

Ginnie Mae *See* Government National Mortgage Association.

good faith estimate A disclosure offered by the lender within three days of a formal loan application that shows all fees associated with the purchase and any required impounds for escrow of taxes, insurance, or mortgage insurance.

Government National Mortgage Association (GNMA) Known as Ginnie Mae, this government-controlled agency supports the purchase and sale of FHA/VA mortgage loans.

grace period A period of time allowable until a payment on a loan is made, with no penalty.

graduated-payment mortgage (GPM) An adjustable-rate mortgage that allows less than the required payment to be made, with the additional unpaid amount being added to the total amount due. This causes negative amortization.

gross income Earnings before taxes and withholdings are subtracted.

Gross National Product (GNP) The value of all goods and services in a particular economic period.

gross profit Earnings before expenses are deducted to arrive at net income.

growing equity mortgage (GEM) A fixed-rate loan that requires lower initial payments than required to pay off the loan in the amortized period, with gradual increases that should coincide with cost-of-living raises as payments rise. It could result in negative amortization.

guaranty A contractual promise by one party to perform on an obligation if another obligated party does not perform.

hazard insurance   Homeowner's insurance protection required to protect the dwelling against natural and unforeseen hazards.

home equity line of credit (HELOC)   A revolving loan usually associated with the prime rate that allows homeowners to use their home's equity as collateral on a loan, with payments normally calculated with minimum interest only and no required principal reduction, usually available for up to 10 years.

home equity loan (HELOAN)   An installment loan that requires the loan against the savings in the home to be repaid in equal installments for a specified period of time, with definite beginning and ending dates.

homeowner's association   The local governing group of owners responsible for managing a cooperating group of owners, as in a condominium complex.

Housing and Urban Development (HUD)   Formed in 1965, this government agency oversees housing issues and legislation for all facets of housing, including homeownership through the FHA.

HUD-1 Settlement Statement   *See* closing statement.

hybrid ARM   A combination fixed-rate and adjustable-rate loan. The loan is fixed for a period of time, and will then become an adjustable rate loan.

impound account   *See* escrow account.

indemnity   An agreement between parties to protect against loss or damage.

index   The money source that drives the movement of an adjustable-loan product, such as the one-three-five year Treasury securities.

indexed rate   The total of the index plus the margin. If the index is 6.55 percent and the margin is 2.75 percent, the indexed rate is 9.3.

inflation   The increase or expansion of an economy over its natural growth.

ingress and egress   The right to enter and pass through, not stay on, a property.

inquiry   A notation on a credit report showing what companies and individuals have had access to the credit history.

inspection   The opportunity to thoroughly examine a home before you continue with the purchase, to determine its condition.

interest   Money charged for the use of money.

interest rate   The rate at which money will be charged for the use of money.

interim financing   A temporary loan put into place until permanent financing, such as a construction loan, is obtained.

investment property   Income-producing real estate purchased to create profit.

investor   A money source available for a lender.

joint tenancy   More than one owner, usually with a survivorship provision stating that the title will automatically transfer to the remaining party without reference to the decedent's will.

judgment   An unpaid, court-ordered repayment obligation.

jumbo loan   A loan amount larger than conforming loan limits established by the FNMA and FHLMC, usually with a slightly higher interest rate than a conforming loan.

land contract   Sale in which the buyer agrees to pay monthly payments to own, but ownership does not transfer until the seller receives all payments.

lease with option to purchase   A rental arrangement in which a portion of the rents paid accumulates toward a down payment for a future purchase.

leasehold   An estate held under a lease for a specified length of time.

lender   A person who advances funds to a borrower, secured by a mortgage or deed in trust.

lender policy   The title insurance policy that protects the mortgagee against claims of ownership on the property. *See* title insurance.

liability   Debt to be repaid.

LIBOR   *See* London Interbank Offered Rate.

lien   A claim against a property for monetary value.

loan   Money given with the expectation of repayment.

loan officer   The employee of a lender whose job it is to provide information and facilitate the loan process.

loan processor   The employee of a lender who assists the loan officer and presents the paperwork for review and approval.

loan-origination fee   Usually calculated at 1 percent of the loan amount and collected as a fee to do business by the lender.

loan-to-value (LTV)   A relationship expressed as a ratio between the property value of the home and the amount of the loan.

lock or lock in   Refers to a commitment when setting the interest rate for the mortgage loan, protecting the rate from rising while the loan is processing and before the loan closing.

London Interbank Offered Rate (LIBOR)   A British monetary policy indicator that is used to guide the movement of some adjustable-rate loans.

loss-payable clause   The ownership clause on a homeowner's insurance policy naming both the borrower and the lender as owners so that if there is a claim, the lender is made aware and can ensure that the work to be completed is taken care of with the proceeds provided by the insurance company.

margin   The amount a lender adds to the index on an adjustable-rate mortgage to establish the interest rate, sometimes noted as the profit margin to the lender.

market data approach   *See* competitive market analysis.

market value   The highest price a buyer will pay and the lowest price a seller will accept for a property at any given time.

mechanic's lien   Work owed to a contractor, secured by the property in the form of an encumbrance to guarantee payment.

mortgage   The piece of paper that secures the property as collateral for repaying the note, or monies borrowed on a real estate transaction. Known also as a deed of trust in some parts of the country.

mortgage banker   Person who originates, approves, and closes loans in his name.

mortgage broker   Originates loans but uses someone else's money. Brokers tend to work for numerous lenders, including banks, mortgage companies, and thrifts.

mortgage correspondent   Originates loans for several lenders, but closes loans in their name and later transfers the ownership to another lender.

mortgage credit certificate (MCC)   A federal program that provides a tax credit for the homeowner for a portion of income tax due and allows the lender to raise the income proportionally to assist the buyer in qualifying for a home loan.

mortgage insurance   *See* FHA mortgage insurance premium and private mortgage insurance (PMI).

mortgage insurance premium (MIP)   *See* FHA mortgage insurance premium.

mortgage servicing   The responsibility of collecting payments, paying taxes and insurances, releasing the lien when paid in full, and initiating foreclosure proceedings if the borrower defaults by the lender or another company, for a fee.

mortgage-backed securities   Securities guaranteed by a group or pool of mortgage loans, with returns that will fluctuate depending upon the performance of the pool, such as loans paid off early or defaulted loans.

mortgagee   The lender in a mortgage transaction.

mortgagor   The borrower in a mortgage transaction.

multifamily dwelling   Two to four units, either owner occupied or investment.

Multiple Listing Service (MLS)   An exclusive service available to members that provides detailed information of properties available for sale.

negative amortization   When the interest rate and payment do not change at the same time, causing the payment to be lower than what should be made to properly pay the mortgage, causing more interest to accrue.

net worth   The difference between total assets and total liabilities.

no-income/no-asset verification (NINA)   A loan option that requires no disclosure of income or assets.

nonassumption clause   A statement in the mortgage prohibiting the transfer of real estate by assumption without the consent of the lender.

nonconforming loans   Loans that do not meet the standard lending requirements of FNMA or FHLMC, whether for property type, loan amount, or loan standards.

note   A signed obligation to repay a debt for a specific amount due at a preset time. It usually provides for interest payments and is secured by a mortgage in the case of a real estate transaction.

occupancy   Refers to who will live in the home and whether they are the owner or tenants.

Office of Thrift Supervision (OTS)   The regulatory agency that oversees the operation of thrifts and savings and loans. *See* Federal Home Loan Bank Board.

open mortgage   Loan that may be prepaid without penalty.

open-ended mortgage   A mortgage that allows the borrower to increase the amount of the loan during the term of the mortgage.

origination fee   *See* loan-origination fee.

owner's title policy   An insurance policy provided to the borrower that gives the buyer a free and clear title from defects dating prior to the date of closing to closing, listing the borrower as the policy beneficiary.

par value   The value of a mortgage without the payment of discount points.

pay off   Remove the balance through sale, principal reduction, or with another lien.

per-diem interest   The lender's daily charge for interest.

permanent interest rate buy-down   When discount points are paid at closing to drive the interest rate down for the life of the loan.

permanent mortgage   A long-term loan rather than an interim loan.

piggyback mortgages   A second lien issued at the same time as a first, to assist in the down payment necessary to complete the transaction.

plat   A map that shows the boundaries of the property in relation to the neighborhood or surrounding area.

pledged-asset mortgage (PAM)   Money placed in an interest-bearing savings account that over time will reduce the cost of the mortgage payment.

points   *See* discount point.

portfolio lender   A lender who makes loans, collects the payments, and uses his or her own funds rather than those available through the secondary market.

power of attorney   Legal paperwork allowing another to act upon your behalf.

preapproval   A mortgage application that allows a borrower to arrange financing in advance of finding a home to purchase, contingent upon the lender's satisfactory review of the property.

preliminary title   A report showing the stipulations of the title before the loan closes.

prepaid expenses   These include escrow items for taxes, insurance, mortgage insurance paid at closing, and interest on the loan from the date of closing through the remainder of the month.

prepayment   The ability to pay extra payments toward the loan to reduce the overall interest on the loan.

prepayment penalty   A fee assessed if a loan is paid in advance of its due date, either in full or as a partial monthly payment.

primary mortgage market   The local contact for the borrower in a lending transaction, such as local banks, savings and loans, and mortgage companies; they often go to the secondary market for the money they are lending to the buyer.

prime lending rate   The going rate of commercial banks and thrifts for consumer loans.

principal   The amount originally borrowed for the loan, excluding the interest.

principal, interest, taxes, insurance (PITI)   The payment acronym describes the entire payment.

private mortgage insurance (PMI) Risk insurance paid by the borrower to protect the lender in case the loan ends in default and later goes into foreclosure. This insurance is required on loans with less than 20 percent down payment.

pro rate To divide in equal shares at loan closing so buyers and sellers have acceptable coverage for such items as taxes and insurance.

proceeds The amount left over, or the immediate sale monies after expenses, such as after the sale of a home.

property tax Municipality assessment based upon the value of the home, paid for community services.

public records Usually local municipality records tracking vital statistics, probate, real estate sales, and so on. These records are available to anyone interested.

purchase agreement The contract between buyer and seller that addresses all the terms and conditions of a purchase transaction, from price to occupancy.

purchase money mortgage Any mortgage that provides cash that will be used toward the down payment of a loan.

quitclaim deed A deed that releases a grantor from a claim to the title of a property without warranty.

radon A colorless, odorless gas in the soil that can enter the structure through the foundation and cause health issues for the occupants.

real estate Land and anything permanently affixed to it, such as buildings and anything in the buildings that is considered real property.

Real Estate Settlement Procedures Act (RESPA) The law requires lenders to provide accurate settlement information within three days of a mortgage application. Also known as a good-faith estimate.

Realtor A professional designation and registered trademark given to a real estate professional who is affiliated with the National Association of Realtors (NAR).

recapture The return of monies that have been used for the purchase after the home has sold and closed.

recast   Change the terms of a loan without rewriting or refinancing the loan, either to correct a defaulted loan issue or to modify a loan payment after a significant principal reduction.

reconveyance   An instrument that transfers the loan from the lender to the borrower when it is satisfied, or paid in full.

recording fees   Charges by a local municipality to register a document for public record.

redemption   Canceling the lien against real estate because it is uncollectible due to foreclosure.

redlining   The practice of discrimination based upon a certain demographic or geographic type, with no regard for the borrower's creditworthiness.

referral   The recommendation of a satisfied party for a service to be performed.

refinance   Rewrite of a loan on the same property to improve the terms or liquidate equity for debt consolidation or home improvements.

Regulation Z   The federal law that sets forth standard disclosure procedures regarding fees and costs to obtain a mortgage using the truth-in-lending disclosure and APR calculations.

reinstatement   To bring back current a mortgage, or restore a veteran's eligibility benefits from a previous home loan to allow him to reuse the entitlement.

reissue rate   Title insurance premium reduction for repeat customers for the same property within a specified time.

release of liability   An instrument that removes the property from the mortgage or lien. It can also remove a borrower from the deed, in the case of a loan assumption.

rescission   The grace period on a refinance after signing to cancel, usually within three days.

reserve   Funds unused after a home purchase that are set aside for contingency in case of future maintenance issues.

residual   Discretionary income remaining after all expenses have been taken into consideration. In the case of a VA home loan, this is one factor considered.

reverse mortgage   For seniors over 62, the lender makes payments of equity back to a homeowner using an acceptable FHA mortgage.

rider   An addendum to the mortgage that specifies a deviation, such as a condominium rider or adjustable-rate mortgage rider that outlines the terms pursuant to the specified loan program.

sales contract   *See* purchase agreement.

satisfaction   Release of the obligation due to a sale or payoff of the balance.

savings and loans   Federally insured institutions originally chartered to promote savings and offer home buyers financing after the Great Depression.

second mortgage   Mortgage made subsequent to another, and taking a secondary lien position.

secondary market   The outlet for lenders to sell loans and recover their capital to lend again.

security interest   An interest or warranty that a lender puts into place to guarantee repayment of their loan.

settlement statement   *See* closing statement.

shared-appreciation mortgage (SAM)   The borrower receives a below-market interest rate in return for sharing earned future appreciation with that party, either the lender or a family member.

sheriff's sale   The process of liquidating bank-held real estate that has been foreclosed upon. Named such because historically a sheriff presided over the sale, which is usually held at the courthouse.

short sale   A sale of property by the lender that may forgive an indebtedness to the borrower. The forgiven amount is treated as income to the borrower and taxed accordingly.

simple interest   Interest computed only on the outstanding principal balance.

Small Business Administration (SBA)   A federal agency authorized to make loans to small businesses for expansion, construction, and even the purchase of land.

subordination agreement   The reinstatement of a lien in a junior position with the approval of the lender.

subprime   Loans for borrowers who may not meet one or all of the conforming loan requirements.

subsidy   A grant to aid with or reduce the cost of a product or service.

surety   One who agrees to be obligated to the debt of another, such as a co-mortgagor.

survey   The measurement of boundaries on a piece of land, showing the dimension and location of adjacent buildings or structures.

sweat equity   The agreement to work in exchange for a reduced down payment on a loan.

swing loan   *See* bridge loan/bridge financing.

teaser rate   A below-market interest rate meant to create curiosity for a potential buyer. The rate will increase to market rate within a designated time.

tenancy by the entirety   An ownership by husband and wife whereby each owns equal parts of the property. Upon the death of one party, the ownership interest automatically transfers to the surviving spouse.

tenancy in common   An undivided ownership in real estate by two parties. The death of one owner does not automatically give the rights of ownership to the surviving party.

tenant in severalty   One who owns property alone, without anyone else being named.

term   A period of time.

title   The written evidence that proves the right of ownership to a specific property.

title insurance   *See* owner's title policy.

title search   An examination of public records to discover information pertinent to the subject property.

truth-in-lending disclosure   Standard disclosure form that details costs of a loan, designed to allow borrowers a standard for comparing different institutions.

underwriting   The analysis of information to determine a borrower's ability to repay an obligation based upon credit, employment, and assets.

usury   Excessive charge of interest as established by law.

VA escape clause   Disclosure signed by all parties stating that the buyer is not held liable to complete the transaction to purchase a home if the appraisal determines the value to be less than the sales price.

VA funding fee   A charge by the Veteran's Administration that can be financed into the loan, covering administrative expenses.

VA loan   A mortgage that has a guarantee by the Veteran's Administration.

variable-rate mortgage (VRM)   *See* adjustable-rate mortgage.

Verification of Deposit (VOD)   Form sent by a lender to a banking institution to verify funds available for the purposes of a mortgage loan.

Verification of Employment (VE)   Form sent by a lender to an employer to verify income and earnings for the repayment of a mortgage loan.

Verification of Mortgage/Rental (VOM/VOR)   Forms sent to a mortgage company or a rental agent to verify the amount and payment history.

warehouse fee   Mortgage company fee to borrow short-term money that, in turn, is lent to the borrower from the secondary market.

wraparound mortgage   An existing mortgage loan is combined with a new mortgage, blending the rates. The payment is made to the new lender, who then forwards the remainder to the original creditor.

Loan Table

To use this chart, find the interest rate of the loan you are considering in the left column and the term of the loan across the top row. Where that row and column intersect, you will find the monthly payment amount for a $1,000 loan. Then multiply that payment by how many thousands you are borrowing.

For example: A 6 percent loan for 30 years is $6 per month per thousand. If you borrow $150,000, then multiply 150 × $6 to get a principal and interest payment of $900.

Monthly Payment per $1,000 of Principal Borrowed at Interest Rates from 2 to 17 Percent over 10- to 40-Year Terms

Rate	10	15	20	25	30	40
2.000%	$9.20	$6.44	$5.06	$4.24	$3.70	$3.03
2.125%	$9.26	$6.49	$5.12	$4.30	$3.76	$3.09
2.250%	$9.31	$6.55	$5.18	$4.36	$3.82	$3.16
2.375%	$9.37	$6.61	$5.24	$4.42	$3.89	$3.23
2.500%	$9.43	$6.67	$5.30	$4.49	$3.95	$3.30
2.625%	$9.48	$6.73	$5.36	$4.55	$4.02	$3.37

continues

Monthly Payment per $1,000 of Principal Borrowed at Interest Rates from 2 to 17 Percent over 10- to 40-Year Terms (continued)

Rate	10	15	20	25	30	40
2.750%	$9.54	$6.79	$5.42	$4.61	$4.08	$3.44
2.875%	$9.60	$6.85	$5.48	$4.68	$4.15	$3.51
3.000%	$9.66	$6.91	$5.55	$4.74	$4.22	$3.58
3.125%	$9.71	$6.97	$5.61	$4.81	$4.28	$3.65
3.250%	$9.77	$7.03	$5.67	$4.87	$4.35	$3.73
3.375%	$9.83	$7.09	$5.74	$4.94	$4.42	$3.80
3.500%	$9.89	$7.15	$5.80	$5.01	$4.49	$3.87
3.625%	$9.95	$7.21	$5.86	$5.07	$4.56	$3.95
3.750%	$10.01	$7.27	$5.93	$5.14	$4.63	$4.03
3.875%	$10.07	$7.33	$5.99	$5.21	$4.70	$4.10
4.000%	$10.12	$7.40	$6.06	$5.28	$4.77	$4.18
4.125%	$10.18	$7.46	$6.13	$5.35	$4.85	$4.26
4.250%	$10.24	$7.52	$6.19	$5.42	$4.92	$4.34
4.375%	$10.30	$7.59	$6.26	$5.49	$4.99	$4.42
4.500%	$10.36	$7.65	$6.33	$5.56	$5.07	$4.50
4.625%	$10.42	$7.71	$6.39	$5.63	$5.14	$4.58
4.750%	$10.48	$7.78	$6.46	$5.70	$5.22	$4.66
4.875%	$10.55	$7.84	$6.53	$5.77	$5.29	$4.74
5.000%	$10.61	$7.91	$6.60	$5.85	$5.37	$4.82
5.125%	$10.67	$7.97	$6.67	$5.92	$5.44	$4.91
5.250%	$10.73	$8.04	$6.74	$5.99	$5.52	$4.99
5.375%	$10.79	$8.10	$6.81	$6.07	$5.60	$5.07
5.500%	$10.85	$8.17	$6.88	$6.14	$5.68	$5.16
5.625%	$10.91	$8.24	$6.95	$6.22	$5.76	$5.24
5.750%	$10.98	$8.30	$7.02	$6.29	$5.84	$5.33
5.875%	$11.04	$8.37	$7.09	$6.37	$5.92	$5.42
6.000%	$11.10	$8.44	$7.16	$6.44	$6.00	$5.50
6.125%	$11.16	$8.51	$7.24	$6.52	$6.08	$5.59

Rate	10	15	20	25	30	40
6.250%	$11.23	$8.57	$7.31	$6.60	$6.16	$5.68
6.375%	$11.29	$8.64	$7.38	$6.67	$6.24	$5.77
6.500%	$11.35	$8.71	$7.46	$6.75	$6.32	$5.85
6.625%	$11.42	$8.78	$7.53	$6.83	$6.40	$5.94
6.750%	$11.48	$8.85	$7.60	$6.91	$6.49	$6.03
6.875%	$11.55	$8.92	$7.68	$6.99	$6.57	$6.12
7.000%	$11.61	$8.99	$7.75	$7.07	$6.65	$6.21
7.125%	$11.68	$9.06	$7.83	$7.15	$6.74	$6.31
7.250%	$11.74	$9.13	$7.90	$7.23	$6.82	$6.40
7.375%	$11.81	$9.20	$7.98	$7.31	$6.91	$6.49
7.500%	$11.87	$9.27	$8.06	$7.39	$6.99	$6.58
7.625%	$11.94	$9.34	$8.13	$7.47	$7.08	$6.67
7.750%	$12.00	$9.41	$8.21	$7.55	$7.16	$6.77
7.875%	$12.07	$9.48	$8.29	$7.64	$7.25	$6.86
8.000%	$12.13	$9.56	$8.36	$7.72	$7.34	$6.95
8.125%	$12.20	$9.63	$8.44	$7.80	$7.42	$7.05
8.250%	$12.27	$9.70	$8.52	$7.88	$7.51	$7.14
8.375%	$12.33	$9.77	$8.60	$7.97	$7.60	$7.24
8.500%	$12.40	$9.85	$8.68	$8.05	$7.69	$7.33
8.625%	$12.47	$9.92	$8.76	$8.14	$7.78	$7.43
8.750%	$12.53	$9.99	$8.84	$8.22	$7.87	$7.52
8.875%	$12.60	$10.07	$8.92	$8.31	$7.96	$7.62
9.000%	$12.67	$10.14	$9.00	$8.39	$8.05	$7.71
9.125%	$12.74	$10.22	$9.08	$8.48	$8.14	$7.81
9.250%	$12.80	$10.29	$9.16	$8.56	$8.23	$7.91
9.375%	$12.87	$10.37	$9.24	$8.65	$8.32	$8.00
9.500%	$12.94	$10.44	$9.32	$8.74	$8.41	$8.10
9.625%	$13.01	$10.52	$9.40	$8.82	$8.50	$8.20
9.750%	$13.08	$10.59	$9.49	$8.91	$8.59	$8.30
9.875%	$13.15	$10.67	$9.57	$9.00	$8.68	$8.39
10.000%	$13.22	$10.75	$9.65	$9.09	$8.78	$8.49
10.125%	$13.28	$10.82	$9.73	$9.18	$8.87	$8.59

continues

Monthly Payment per $1,000 of Principal Borrowed at Interest Rates from 2 to 17 Percent over 10- to 40-Year Terms   (continued)

Rate	10	15	20	25	30	40
10.250%	$13.35	$10.90	$9.82	$9.26	$8.96	$8.69
10.375%	$13.42	$10.98	$9.90	$9.35	$9.05	$8.79
10.500%	$13.49	$11.05	$9.98	$9.44	$9.15	$8.89
10.625%	$13.56	$11.13	$10.07	$9.53	$9.24	$8.98
10.750%	$13.63	$11.21	$10.15	$9.62	$9.33	$9.08
10.875%	$13.70	$11.29	$10.24	$9.71	$9.43	$9.18
11.000%	$13.78	$11.37	$10.32	$9.80	$9.52	$9.28
11.125%	$13.85	$11.44	$10.41	$9.89	$9.62	$9.38
11.250%	$13.92	$11.52	$10.49	$9.98	$9.71	$9.48
11.375%	$13.99	$11.60	$10.58	$10.07	$9.81	$9.58
11.500%	$14.06	$11.68	$10.66	$10.16	$9.90	$9.68
11.625%	$14.13	$11.76	$10.75	$10.26	$10.00	$9.78
11.750%	$14.20	$11.84	$10.84	$10.35	$10.09	$9.88
11.875%	$14.27	$11.92	$10.92	$10.44	$10.19	$9.98
12.000%	$14.35	$12.00	$11.01	$10.53	$10.29	$10.08
12.125%	$14.42	$12.08	$11.10	$10.62	$10.38	$10.19
12.250%	$14.49	$12.16	$11.19	$10.72	$10.48	$10.29
12.375%	$14.56	$12.24	$11.27	$10.81	$10.58	$10.39
12.500%	$14.64	$12.33	$11.36	$10.90	$10.67	$10.49
12.625%	$14.71	$12.41	$11.45	$11.00	$10.77	$10.59
12.750%	$14.78	$12.49	$11.54	$11.09	$10.87	$10.69
12.875%	$14.86	$12.57	$11.63	$11.18	$10.96	$10.79
13.000%	$14.93	$12.65	$11.72	$11.28	$11.06	$10.90
13.125%	$15.00	$12.73	$11.80	$11.37	$11.16	$11.00
13.250%	$15.08	$12.82	$11.89	$11.47	$11.26	$11.10
13.375%	$15.15	$12.90	$11.98	$11.56	$11.36	$11.20
13.500%	$15.23	$12.98	$12.07	$11.66	$11.45	$11.30
13.625%	$15.30	$13.07	$12.16	$11.75	$11.55	$11.40

Rate	10	15	20	25	30	40
13.750%	$15.38	$13.15	$12.25	$11.85	$11.65	$11.51
13.875%	$15.45	$13.23	$12.34	$11.94	$11.75	$11.61
14.000%	$15.53	$13.32	$12.44	$12.04	$11.85	$11.71
14.125%	$15.60	$13.40	$12.53	$12.13	$11.95	$11.81
14.250%	$15.68	$13.49	$12.62	$12.23	$12.05	$11.92
14.375%	$15.75	$13.57	$12.71	$12.33	$12.15	$12.02
14.500%	$15.83	$13.66	$12.80	$12.42	$12.25	$12.12
14.625%	$15.90	$13.74	$12.89	$12.52	$12.35	$12.22
14.750%	$15.98	$13.83	$12.98	$12.61	$12.44	$12.33
14.875%	$16.06	$13.91	$13.08	$12.71	$12.54	$12.43
15.000%	$16.13	$14.00	$13.17	$12.81	$12.64	$12.54
15.125%	$16.21	$14.08	$13.26	$12.91	$12.74	$12.64
15.250%	$16.29	$14.17	$13.35	$13.00	$12.84	$12.74
15.375%	$16.36	$14.25	$13.45	$13.10	$12.94	$12.84
15.500%	$16.44	$14.34	$13.54	$13.20	$13.05	$12.94
15.625%	$16.52	$14.43	$13.63	$13.30	$13.15	$13.05
15.750%	$16.60	$14.51	$13.73	$13.39	$13.25	$13.15
15.875%	$16.67	$14.60	$13.82	$13.49	$13.35	$13.25
16.000%	$16.75	$14.69	$13.91	$13.59	$13.45	$13.36
16.125%	$16.83	$14.77	$14.01	$13.69	$13.55	$13.46
16.250%	$16.91	$14.86	$14.10	$13.79	$13.65	$13.56
16.375%	$16.99	$14.95	$14.19	$13.88	$13.75	$13.67
16.500%	$17.06	$15.04	$14.29	$13.98	$13.85	$13.77
16.625%	$17.14	$15.13	$14.38	$14.08	$13.95	$13.87
16.750%	$17.22	$15.21	$14.48	$14.18	$14.05	$13.98
16.875%	$17.30	$15.30	$14.57	$14.28	$14.16	$14.08
17.000%	$17.38	$15.39	$14.67	$14.38	$14.26	$14.18

Index